Religion and the Social Sciences

Religion and the Social Sciences

Conversations with Robert Bellah
and Christian Smith

EDITED BY

R. R. Reno
&
Barbara McClay

CASCADE *Books* · Eugene, Oregon

RELIGION AND THE SOCIAL SCIENCES
Conversations with Robert Bellah and Christian Smith

Cascade Books
An Imprint of Wipf and Stock Publishers
199 W. 8th Ave., Suite 3
Eugene, OR 97401

www.wipfandstock.com

ISBN 13: 978-1-4982-3644-7

Cataloguing-in-Publication Data

Religion and the social sciences : conversations with Robert Bellah and Christian Smith / edited by R. R. Reno and Barbara Mcclay.

xvii + 118 p. ; 23 cm. Includes bibliographical references.

ISBN 13: 978-1-62564-172-4

1. Sociology—Religion. 2. Sociology—Philosophy. I. Reno, R. R. II. McClay, Barbara. III. Title.

BD450 R425 2015

Manufactured in the U.S.A.   07/22/2015

In Memoriam: Robert Bellah

Contents

Preface

THE CHAPTERS IN THIS book began as papers drafted to stimulate discussion at two day-and-a-half-long seminars sponsored by the Institute on Religion and Public Life, publisher of *First Things*. Funded by the Religion and Innovation in Human Affairs project of the Historical Society, the first seminar focused on Robert Bellah's remarkable synthesis of evolutionary science, social science, and religious studies, *Religion in Human Evolution*. It met in New York on December 10–11, 2012. The second met on April 8–9, also in New York. This group of scholars discussed Christian Smith's program for social science, *What is a Person?*

The written word is no substitute for the vitality of a living conversation, and the two seminars were nothing if not lively. However, it is my hope that these critical essays and responses by Robert Bellah and Christian Smith give readers a sense of how theologians and philosophers engage the social sciences. This is an important conversation, not just for contemporary academic culture, but for our society as well.

On behalf of the Institute on Religion and Public Life and all the participants in the two seminars, I would like to thank Donald Yerxa, director of Religion and Innovation in Human Affairs. I would also like to thank Robert Bellah and Christian Smith. The paper writers and seminar participants spoke their minds, which sometimes meant sharply worded criticism of their books. Both responded with an enviable combination of intellectual confidence and personal good will.

I also would like to thank staff members here at *First Things* for their work in coordinating the seminars and bringing this volume into shape for publication. A special thanks goes to Lauren Wilson and Bianca Czaderna.

Finally, a special thanks goes to Barbara McClay, my coeditor. She worked with all the authors and her fine editorial skills contributed a great deal to the success of this book.

–R. R. Reno

Introduction

IN MY TWENTY YEARS of teaching undergraduates, more often than not it was a class in the social sciences that challenged the faith of students, not a class in biology. Most potent was biblical studies, a modern tradition that gave rise to some of the most important techniques of social and cultural analysis by applying them to the Bible. In these classes pious students felt themselves undercut. What they had imagined as solid, fixed, and authoritative became a plastic reality. Moral truths, religious doctrines, religious experiences? These are manifestations of hidden historical, cultural, and psychological dynamics. So papal authority reflects an institutional need for fixed boundaries; doctrines about the Virgin Mary need to be understood in terms of a larger context of religious exaltations and domestications of the feminine; and so forth.

It's not hard to see why faith finds itself challenged by modern social science. Christianity and Judaism privilege sacred texts as the ultimate horizon for our historical, social, and moral imaginations. By contrast, Freud saw monotheism as emerging out of an Oedipal psychodrama enacted in the distant past. Weber interpreted religion in terms of an oscillation between charisma and institutionalization. These and other theories have their secular critics, but the general structure of explanation was (and remains) constant. As a modern tradition of inquiry, social science wants to get underneath religion, as it were, explaining it in terms of something more fundamental.

As was argued by Ludwig Feuerbach, one of the forefathers of sociology of religion, God is not the source of all reality. On the contrary, he is the projection of our conception of idealized human reality, and the source of all culture is that conception—or, better, our capacity to form such a conception. Like everything else, God is the upshot of our uniquely human culture-making potency. Almost all social scientists make this claim, even if only implicitly.

Need it be so? Is social science necessarily on a collision course with traditional modes of religious understanding? It was with this question in mind that we gathered two groups of scholars to participate in seminars to discuss two ambitious books of sociology: Robert Bellah's *Religion in Human Evolution*, and Christian Smith's *What Is a Person?* Seminar participants were from different disciplines, though heavily tilted toward philosophy and theology. We met for a day and a half of intense discussion, focusing on papers and responses prepared in advance, and allowing time for Bellah and Smith to respond. The results are before you in this volume.

The seminar to discuss Bellah's *Religion in Human Evolution* met in New York in December 2012. Bellah's work is a big, remarkable book with an important argument that is for the most part congenial to religious people. By Bellah's reckoning, a full assessment of the evidence for biological evolution shows that human development involves more than genetic mutation and the struggle for survival. Animal play, which is widely observed, creates an experienced reality that operates on different principles. The upshot is a primeval pluralism, a prehistoric division of consciousness in animals that creates a tension.

It's across this difference between survival and play that distinctively human cognitive characteristics emerge: imagination, intentions, and eventually, cultural forms. Religious ritual, argues Bellah, is a kind of play, and the imaginative possibility of human modes outside the struggle for existences both feeds and is fed by religious beliefs and practices.

In a sense, therefore, Feuerbach was right. We are culture-making animals. But Bellah's remarkable engagement with evolutionary theory reminds us that we were not always so. We were at some point *just* survival-seeking organisms. It was the liminal experiences of play—moments of freedom in which our prehuman ancestors transcended the gritty game our DNA plays to maximize its chances of survival—that created the possibility of our evolution into culture-making animals.

But that means, of course, that we do not "create" religion, as Feuerbach suggests. On the contrary, in its most primitive form, religion—play—creates us. Put differently, when we go "underneath" our inherited moral and religious beliefs with the techniques of socials science, we find their most primitive forms, not explained by supposedly deeper psychological or cultural dynamics, but rather as the explanation for what makes humans distinctively human.

The seminar featured a number of essays and responses. Three were revised and published as a symposium in *First Things* (June/July 2013), along with substantive response by Robert Bellah, which built upon his oral remarks during the seminar. We have kept them in a unified group in this volume.

In "From Play to Freedom" Francesca Murphy takes up Bellah's emphasis on play, reading *Religion in Human Evolution* as a fitting sequel to and a deepening of Johan Huizinga's *Homo Ludens: A Study of the Play Element in Culture*. To a great extent our secular intellectual culture has accepted, at least tacitly, the view that human behavior stems from the survival game played by our selfish genes. What Bellah shows, however, is that culture emerges in the zone of play. We are of course deeply and profoundly formed by inherited modes of thinking—what Bellah calls "conserved core processes"—but those modes have an open-ended quality that allows us to say that we are both created by and create culture. For this reason Murphy concludes that Bellah articulates an anthropology of freedom, and the mode of social science he advances offers a congenial resource to Christian theologians.

Paul Griffiths is less enthusiastic. In "Impossible Pluralism" he argues that Bellah's book—and by implication the social scientific project taken as a whole—collides with Christian theology. Both purport to provide an ultimate explanation of the origins and ends of life, "metanarratives" in his terminology, and so must compete in the end. We'll either adopt a social scientific theory of everything, in which theology plays a subordinate role, if any, or a theological account of reality, in which the traditions of modern social science are subordinate. Metanarratives brook no competitors. There is no third, mediating possibility.

We should read Thomas Joseph White's contribution to the seminar, "Sociology as Theology," as performing what Griffiths asserts: the primacy of theology. He argues that *Religion in Human Evolution* should be read as an exemplary text of liberal Protestant theology. It follows in the tradition of Friedrich Schleiermacher, and especially Ernst Troeltsch, showing how religion expresses a universal and natural human potency for transcendence. In Bellah's telling, a universal history of humanity told with the tools of modern science reinterprets the premodern dogmatism of traditional religion as reflecting a deep human truth, and in that sense builds theology "from the bottom up."

It was Griffiths's fierce challenge and the provocation of White's denomination of his project as liberal Protestant theology that dominated the December 2012 seminar, evoking from Robert Bellah forceful and multi-faceted responses that asserted the independence of social science from theology and—more importantly and persistently—insisted on the possibility of interpretive pluralism. At a critical juncture on the second day of the seminar, Bellah asked a probing question: Can one believe in more than one religion? A number of participants gave measured, nuanced responses that allowed for the benefits of interreligious and cross-cultural dialogue and analysis, but nevertheless added up to a "no." Bellah thought this answer overdetermined by a theoretical monism of the sort Griffiths theorizes. Can't we in fact entertain and enter into alternative accounts of reality? It's an arresting question, one that embodies a noble ideal: the intellectual and spiritual life is enriched by a participatory, empathetic understanding of a diverse range of views. This ideal animates the modern university at its best.

This collision—Griffiths's relentless either/or over and against Bellah's cognitive pluralism—helped me see our intellectual and cultural options more clearly. Surely, we have minds plastic enough to enter into world views different from our own. And surely, that's a capacity to encourage, for it enriches us in many ways. But just as surely, our minds are deepened by love's abandoning commitment. Love's knowledge is in many ways blind, because it sees all things in the beloved. And if I must choose between enrichment and abandonment, it's the latter that seems to hold out the most promise, not only for our souls, but for our minds as well. The committed intellect is a penetrating intellect.

The other papers presented at the seminar raise important issues as well, rounding out the seminar's theological engagement with social science. Lenn Goodman's "Ritual and Religion" offers a detailed critical discussion of Bellah's appropriations of evolutionary theory. In "An Offensive Book" Philip Gorski situates *Religion in Human Evolution* in the larger context of contemporary sociology. Edward Feser challenges the interpretive authority of modern social science in "Natural Theology, Revealed Theology, Liberal Theology."

In April 2013, many of the same participants gathered to discuss Christian Smith's *What is a Person?* This programmatic book seeks to introduce a robust concept of the human person into the theory and practice of contemporary social science. Smith sees tendencies in two directions in most scholarship today. The first restricts human reality to what is measurable—a reductive, positivist empiricism. The second assumes a hermeneutical constructivism in which what we experience as human beings gets interpreted as products of socialization. In both cases, the social scientific view of the human person becomes impoverished. Our lives as free, reflective, relational persons are either ignored or get interpreted away.

Against these tendencies, which he examines in detail in different streams of social theory, Smith outlines an alternative: critical realism. In this approach social science fully acknowledges the biological, psychological, and social components of human existence, but sees them contributing to the life-world of a human person who is more than the sum of these components. In other words, we can gain insights from neuroscience, sociobiology, analysis of patterns of socialization, and much more, but we must see them as shaping and refining our understandings (thus the *critical* part of critical realism) rather than providing an exhaustive account of human persons who exist as more than an array of component parts (thus the *realism* part of critical realism).

As is the case in Bellah's *Religion in Human Evolution*, the concept of emergence plays an important role in Smith's critical realism, allowing him to offer an account of how the reality of the human person is intimately connected but not reducible to its powers, capacities, and relations. We are most definitely animals—instinctual, social, rational, and more—but we're a distinct kind of animal, and that distinctness is best thought of in terms of the concept of person.

The seminar was less contentious than the earlier one that focused on *Religion in Human Evolution*. The theological contributions by Phillip Cary ("The Person Before God") and the response by David Yeago ("Revelation's Nature") advanced a nuanced argument for the priority of theology over social science. Cary outlines the way in which Christian theology shaped the meaning of the concept of person in ways that resist any reduction to powers or capacities. However, instead of emergence, Cary sees the crucial concept defining personhood as relation or role. For the human being it is our relation to God. One might say, therefore, that he outlines an account of the source of personhood by way of bestowal—"Let us make man in our image and likeness"—rather than emergence. This does not contradict the substance of Smith's program for the renewal of social science, but it throws into sharp relief the limits of a purely secular approach to the human person.

Yeago reflects on the social and historical significance of Cary's theological account of person. The pathologies of contemporary social science rightly critiqued by Smith are perhaps best understood as the consequences of post-Christian Western culture. Wounded by sin, our reason can see but dimly the true nature of reality, including the reality of the human person. But revelation illuminates reason, guiding us toward the insights of Smith's critical reason. Can we then be optimistic about a social scientific culture disinterested in and often hostile to Christian teaching? Yeago thinks not, though he certainly hopes Smith's critical realism will restrain the distempers of contemporary social theory, if not cure them. We need divine grace and a renewed theological imagination to overturn the antihuman tendencies in our present-day academic culture.

In "On Being Human" Candace Vogler offers a "friendly philosopher's addendum." She suggests that Smith's critical realism requires a dose of Aristotle and Aquinas. *Emergence* is something of a weasel word, a way of demonstrating empirical bona fides while getting something more than what's measurable. While certainly better than a reductive view, it would be better to start with what we actually see and know, which are human beings, full stop. According to Vogler, therefore, we should be empirical in a more radical sense, basing our social science in what we observe as flourishing human life. A moral component—what humanizes?—needs to be built into the starting point of social science.

David Novak agrees and presses a theological point. It is plainly the case that human beings are religious animals, as Aristotle recognized, making contemplation of God the highest good. It would indeed be revolutionary if contemporary social science even allowed (much less endorsed) such a view.

Is social science really in such a bad state? Does it need critical realism in order to be effective and humanizing, as Smith claims? James Rogers thinks not. We don't need to have the whole reality of the human person in view when we undertake social scientific study. In fact, he argues, we can't. Some sort of reductionism becomes inevitable if we're to focus our inquiries and constrain variables sufficiently to produce useful theories. Just as the astrophysicist has to think about the heavens only in one respect, ignoring the full sweep of the night sky, so the social scientist needs to focus on one or two dimensions of human behavior and motivation. Therefore, instead of being pernicious, reductionism is justified as an "analytical convenience," and social scientists should modestly pursue slices of reality rather than trying to assemble a view of the whole. It's a view Stephen Meredith largely endorses, reminding us that for the view of the whole we need philosophy, not science.

In his "Reply to My Critics," Smith accepts Vogler's friendly amendment, but defends the concept of emergence as the best way to defend humanism in today's academic culture. Aristotle may offer a more philosophically elegant solution, but at the price of currency in contemporary debates. Theology is even less likely to gain traction, which is why Smith expresses appreciation for the insights of theologians, but little inclination to follow their theological leads.

But the main force of his reply is directed at Rogers and his defense of reductionism. Yes, of course we need conceptual focus and abstraction to bring precision to our work. But such focus is quite different from the reductive move, which is covertly metaphysical, sliding from what's methodologically necessary to what's "real."

The detail and urgency of Smith's rebuttal of Rogers reveals an important decision for religious intellectuals to make about social science, and perhaps about secular academic study taken as a whole. Rogers knows that lots of bad social science is being done, just as lots of useless papers are being written in comparative literature and trivial experiments are being conducted in the natural sciences. Sloth, blindness, self-deception, groupthink: it's the human condition. But he's largely satisfied with today's social scientific practice, at least when done well. It provides a modest but real margin of insight into human motivation and behavior. Social scientists sometimes say true things about this or that aspect of the human condition, and for that we should be grateful rather than resenting their field's limitations.

By contrast, Smith views today's social science as promoting a crimped, crabbed view of what life is about, thus reinforcing the inhumane tendencies in postmodern culture—and, in some cases, conceiving and gestating them. In Rogers he sees a temptation: that a certain kind of theoretical elegance may satisfy us, or that small gains in understanding will palliate our larger, unnecessary ignorance about what it means to be human. We should be more ambitious, both for the sake of intellectual fulfillment and to combat the incipient nihilism of postmodern academic culture. We need to venture big truths about the human condition—claims based on disciplined scientific inquiry—even at the risk of theoretical inelegance, even at the risk of outrunning empirical verification.

Whether we cast our lots with Rogers or Smith depends a great deal on our intuitions about the limits of reason. There is in Rogers a strong Augustinian streak. The university is part of the city of man, and therefore Christian scholars should have modest expectations. As Augustine argued for political realism satisfied with the merely relative peace of the earthly city, Rogers argues for an academic realism satisfied with the merely relative understandings of a reductive scientific method. Only the heavenly city governed by God's revelation can reliably provide us with the larger, deeper truths about the human condition. By contrast, there's a good bit of Thomism in Smith's approach. Reason can't substitute for revelation, but it has a natural integrity that takes us to the forecourts of divine truth. We should not be satisfied with the meager, anti-metaphysical skepticism of our present academic culture. Our disciplines of study can carry us much further, much higher, enriching our religious understandings and making them more fruitful—not just for us, but for society as whole.

Today, the social sciences often train us to be just technicians. Some disciplines promise to make us expert diagnosticians of the soul (psychology); others, mechanics able to tune up the marketplace (economics) or realign society (the wide variety of disciplines falling under "public policy"). This evolution in the direction of technocratic expertise isn't surprising. Our lives are to a great degree organized by bureaucracies, corporate structures, and consumer culture. We need people able to push therapeutic levers here or turn the screws of incentives there. The machinery of modern life needs its maintenance men.

However contested and inconclusive these seminars may have been, they were undoubtedly about matters far more significant. The relations between religious ways of knowing and social science are difficult, and these two seminars suggest that they will remain so. Religions, or at least monotheistic ones, make imperial claims that always threaten the modern social scientific presumption that reason's methods get us to the bottom of things. I don't see that tension going away. Moreover, love's knowledge will always bridle at the temptations to polytheism always implicit in warm affirmations of pluralism. Finally, the conditions that make Aristotle so indigestible for nearly all social scientists today—to say nothing of theology—as well as the great chasm that separates Rogers from Smith, seem insuperable, at least by the usual methods of academic persuasion.

We can't transform our deepest intellectual prejudices and aspirations with new research or better arguments. Many important concepts and arguments are at stake in these essays, all of them well worth sorting out and debating. But as is always the case when fundamental truths about the human condition is on the table, as Pascal both rued and relished, the heart has its reasons that reason doesn't know.

– R. R. Reno

List of Contributors

Robert Bellah (February 23, 1927–July 30, 2013) was an American sociologist, and the Elliott Professor of Sociology, as well as Professor Emeritus, at the University of California, Berkeley.

Phillip Cary is Professor of Philosophy at Eastern University. His most recent book is *Good News for Anxious Christians: 10 Practical Things You DON'T Have to Do* (Grand Rapids: Brazos, 2010).

Edward Feser is Associate Professor of Philosophy at Pasadena City College. His most recent book is *Scholastic Metaphysics: A Contemporary Introduction* (Neunkirchen-Seelscheid, Germany: Editions Scholasticae, 2014).

Lenn Goodman is Professor of Philosophy and Andrew W. Mellon Professor in the Humanities at Vanderbilt University. His most recent book is *Religious Pluralism and Values in the Public Sphere* (Cambridge: Cambridge University Press, 2014).

Philip Gorski is Professor of Sociology at Yale University. His most recent book is *The Post-Secular Question: Religion in Contemporary Society* (New York: NYU Press, 2012).

Paul Griffiths is Warren Professor of Catholic Theology at Duke Divinity School. His latest book is *Decreation: The Last Things of All Creatures* (Waco, TX: Baylor University Press, 2014).

Stephen Meredith is Professor in the Department of Pathology, the Department of Biochemistry and Molecular Biology, and the College of the University of Chicago.

Francesca Murphy is Professor of Systematic Theology at the University of Notre Dame. Her forthcoming book is *Illuminating Faith: An Invitation to Theology* (London: Bloomsbury, 2015).

David Novak is Professor of Philosophy and J. Richard and Dorothy Shiff Chair of Jewish Studies at the University of Toronto. His forthcoming book is *Zionism and Judaism: A New Theory* (Cambridge: Cambridge University Press, 2015).

James Rogers is Associate Professor of Political Science at Texas A & M University. His most recent book is *Institutional Games and the Supreme Court* (Charlottesville, VA: University of Virginia Press, 2006).

Christian Smith is the William R. Kenan Jr. Professor of Sociology at the University of Notre Dame. His forthcoming book is *To Flourish or Destruct: A Personalist Theory of Human Goods, Motivations, Failure, and Evil* (Chicago: University of Chicago Press, 2015).

Candace Vogler is the David B. and Clara E. Stern Professor of Philosophy and Professor in the College at the University of Chicago. Her most recent book is *Reasonably Vicious* (Cambridge, MA: Harvard University Press, 2002).

Thomas Joseph White, O.P., is Director of the Thomistic Institute and Associate Professor of Systematic Theology at the Dominican House of Studies. His forthcoming book is *The Incarnate Lord: A Thomistic Study in Christology* (Washington, DC: The Catholic University of America Press, 2015).

David Yeago is Professor of Systematic Theology and Ethics at Trinity School for Ministry and the North American Lutheran Seminary. He is the series editor of *Knowing the Triune God: The Work of the Spirit in the Practices of the Church* (Grand Rapids: Eerdmans, 2001).

PART I

Religion and Human Evolution

Robert Bellah

I.1 From Play to Freedom

Francesca Aran Murphy

AT THE BEGINNING OF the eighteenth century, Immanuel Kant contended that struggle is the motive force of human civilization. Through his successors, especially Hegel, the somewhat oxymoronic idea of armed combat as the motor of civilization came to permeate German high culture and soon Western thinking as a whole. Evolutionism, the idea that fit and lasting species originate through success in competing for food and territory, is a vulgarized version of this high-German myth of creative struggle. This myth has proven tenacious, perhaps because it ties in with certain of our deepest intuitions, such as the sense of our human freedom.

In 1938, the Dutch scholar Johan Huizinga wrote a book called *Homo Ludens: A Study of the Play Element in Culture*. He saw all too clearly where the Prussian adulation for armed combat was going. A few paragraphs added to the second edition, published in 1944 when he was imprisoned in a Nazi detention camp, indicate that he proposed his theory of *homo ludens* as an alternative, and an antidote, to the German idealist theory of war as the root of civilization.

The great cultural historian Jacob Burckhardt had proposed in the previous century that ancient Greece was really great when it had *real* war and genuine warriors: from this it degenerated into a merely "agonal" civilization, with its Olympics and drama competitions, and finally ended in decadence. Against this account of the decline of warrior culture, Huizinga argued that Greece had not moved from battle to play, but that its culture had developed from the beginning in "play-like contest,"[1] in "an almost childlike play-sense expressing itself in various play-forms . . . all rooted in ritual and productive of culture by allowing the innate human need of

1. Huizinga, *Homo Ludens*, 75.

rhythm, harmony, change, alternation, contrast and climax, etc., to unfold in full richness."[2] Associated with this sense of play

> is a spirit that strives for honor, dignity, superiority, and beauty. Magic and mystery, heroic longings, the foreshadowings of music, sculpture and logic all seek form and expression in noble play. . . . In play, therefore, the antithetical and agonistic basis of civilization is given from the start, for play is older and more original than civilization.[3]

Huizinga describes play as pretend combat, and as the source of culture, including its war-making dimensions, not its degeneration. Man is not the animal who fights best, and thus survives, but an animal who plays for the sheer joy of it, and thus thrives. Huizinga sees all cultural forms as emerging from such pretend struggles. For instance, poetry arises from riddling contests and mythology from mimetic, "danced-out" (in Bellah's words) enactments of conflicts. His alternative to the mythologizing of the survival-of-the-fittest idea is not to deny that struggle makes any contribution to the progress of culture, but rather to propose that *unbloody* struggle is the seed of all human sacramental ritual and cultural achievement.

I didn't know much about the history of philosophy when I first read *Homo Ludens* as an undergraduate. I owe to Huizinga a mental picture of communal play as the exercise of freedom within a structure of law and form. That helped me to understand what a sacrament is and in particular what the sacrifice of the Mass is. And thus the book led me to begin to consider religion as an objective and public phenomenon. It might seem like a long step from play to the sacrifice of the Mass. But Huizinga quotes Plato, in the *Laws*: "Man is made God's plaything, and that is the best part of him."[4] Plato continues, "Life must be lived as play, playing certain games, making sacrifices, singing and dancing, and then a man will be able to propitiate the gods, and defend himself against his enemies, and win in the contest."[5]

Robert Bellah, in *Religion in Human Evolution: From the Paleolithic to the Axial Age*, pays his respects to this same passage from Plato, and affirms that Huizinga led him back to it. *Religion in Human Evolution* is, as it were, a more scientifically informed version of *Homo Ludens*. Bellah

2. Ibid., 75.
3. Ibid.
4. Plato, *Laws*, 7.796.
5. Ibid.

argues that play is among the elemental "core processes" that enabled the first human beings to become human. "Play is a new kind of capacity, with a very large potentiality of developing more capacities . . . , some of them quite extraordinary."[6]

It was the evolved capacity for play that enabled our first ancestors then to evolve the capacity for symbolic speech and for ritual. They played games that led them to ornament themselves, "dance out" stories, and begin to use language symbolically. Each capacity emerged out of and was embedded in the earliest "core processes," as Bellah calls them: first "self-domestication" or, effectively, familial love, and then, as a result, "a childhood free enough to create intricate and innovative forms of play."[7]

Religion in Human Evolution is important when countless scholars and popular writers describe every cultural phenomenon and pattern of human behavior in evolutionary terms because its account of an emergent humanity positively requires the exercise of freedom. This idea too goes right back to *Homo Ludens*, where Huizinga argues that "play only becomes possible . . . when an influx of *mind* breaks down the absolute determinism of the cosmos." As he puts it, "Child and animal play because they enjoy playing, and therein precisely lies their freedom."[8] Likewise, Bellah argues that play is the free generation of an "alternative reality" outside of the reality in which the struggle for existence is paramount. Unlike activities oriented toward survival, "play is something 'done for its own sake.'" It is "spontaneous and voluntary" and "not a means to an end."[9]

Today everything from aesthetic beauty to romantic love gets translated into the conniving inventiveness of our selfish genes. In such a climate, Bellah's book could intrigue young people and others as *Homo Ludens* intrigued me. And perhaps more so. Many want to understand the implications of modern biology for a larger view of the human person than selfish-gene theory and similar ideas provide. At the same time, we want to take human freedom seriously—including the radical freedom of living for the sake of the transcendent. In other words, we're looking for accounts of religion that factor in evolution without being simplistically reductionist. Bellah's book offers just such an account. He places religion within the story

6. Bellah, *Religion in Human Evolution*, 80.
7. Ibid., 88.
8. Huizinga, *Homo Ludens*, 8.
9. Bellah, *Religion in Human Evolution*, 77.

of human evolution while leaving open the question of whether or not it is a wholly natural phenomenon.

Whatever one thinks of the details of his argument, Bellah is surely pointing us in the right direction. Freedom is an obstacle to reductionist naturalism: we know as a kind of experiential first principle that we are free. Freedom is a datum in the light of which we know all else about ourselves. Play is an expression of this freedom. Bellah contends that freedom as expressed in play, playful freedom, steps outside functional evolutionary competition. People can refuse to be persuaded that human beings play just for the fun of it. But it is powerful evidence in favor of his view that we take so much pleasure in the exercise of playful freedom, strongly suggesting that such freedom is a fulfillment of human nature. So I would say that he is on the right track in seeing ritual as an exercise of playful freedom.

Bellah doesn't go all the way with Plato's *Laws*. If he had, he might have developed a richer idea of freedom. Plato thinks that men and women play because we were made to do so by the gods. Playing is not just an escape from material determination or a rest from the daily evolutionary struggle. It is more, even, than the creation of alternative realities, like Bilbo's riddles, in which to take joy. If Plato is right, playing is the fulfillment of our human nature, what we were made by the gods to do. But Bellah is content with the Kantian conception of freedom as *freedom from* determination or strife, whereas a Platonist would want to press on to the idea of freedom as freedom *for* the fulfillment of our natures as "playthings" of the divine. If one aims to defeat evolutionism from within, one has to go all the way with Plato, as I think Huizinga did.

Even though Bellah limits himself to a narrow and Kantian conception of freedom, reflecting, perhaps, the limitations of the modern way of thinking that shapes our philosophical imaginations, his account of religion as the exercise of free playfulness should be given due credit and taken further. The only time I ever saw Richard Dawkins reduced to stuttering silence was when an Irish philosopher repeatedly asked him about human freedom. Dawkins was left saying "I don't *care* about freedom," because he could not deny that these human DNA carriers experience it. Without any other presuppositions, every person in the audience knew he experienced the exercise of freedom.

Christian theologians, myself included, can get very angry with moderns for defining the term "freedom" in the wrong way. This can lead us to forget what an explosive datum freedom is, in and of itself, no matter how well- or ill-defined it is by our dominant philosophical assumptions. As shown by the Vatican II *Declaration on Religious Freedom*, a little vagueness about the precise meaning of freedom goes a long way in exposing common ground between Christians and nonbelievers.

Perhaps the most fundamental affirmation of freedom comes in Bellah's idea of conserved core processes. This concept allows us to identify structures or patterns internal to organisms that exercise ongoing influence over the evolutionary process. The implications are dramatic: "Instead of lumbering robots, organisms are actors in the process of evolution." In other words, as a species, we exercise some influence over our own development. As he puts it, "We are embedded in a very deep biological . . . history. That history does not determine us, because organisms from the very beginning, and increasingly with each new capacity, have influenced their own fate."[10]

In addition to introducing freedom in the story of our humanity, Bellah also offends against a materialist orthodoxy because he draws on Lamarck's idea that acquired tendencies can be inherited, which means that culture isn't epiphenomenal to the evolution of *homo sapiens*, but is in fact a constituent part. Scientists may think he is skating on thin ice here. But human beings are the only animals who can create traditions, and who are to an extent created by traditions, perhaps even at a deep, biological level.

So again, with his cultural Lamarckianism, Bellah is articulating the principles of a cultural anthropology based on the premise that human beings are free. To the extent that we create and are created by traditions, there is an element of free self-creation integral to what it means to be human. Human evolution must, to an extent, be in human hands, and in human minds. *To an extent*: certainly human beings are not plastic to be engineered in any way we choose.

However controversial among evolutionary scientists, something like Lamarckianism is theologically unavoidable, for it is a presupposition of the Christian doctrine of the fall. If we assume that original sin is not passed on precisely genetically, but *is* transmitted from generation to generation, one has to say that human beings are free to alter human nature, and to do so in a radical way. In *Principles of Catholic Theology*, Joseph Ratzinger writes that "the origin of 'humanity' coincides in time with the origin of man's capacity for tradition."[11]

---

10. Ibid., 83.

11. Ratzinger, *Principles of Catholic Theology*, 89.

On that basis, "Original sin, then, would mean this: The *humanum* is rooted in tradition, to the beginnings of which there belongs, above all, the ability to hear the Other (whom we call God). . . . From the start, not only this ability to hear and this actual hearing but also sin were constitutive in the formation of subjects in whom tradition would inhere—a kind of formation that is itself constitutive of mankind per se."[12]

And one need not say that damage to human nature is the only way in which human beings can cause their nature to evolve. We are capable of transmitting developments for good as well as evil. The gospel is a tradition that Christ promises will become constitutive of our humanity. We have the freedom to transmit the living Word, and we do so by allowing ourselves to be formed by it so deeply that it becomes constitutive of us.

It's quite impossible, of course, for an orthodox Christian theologian to buy into Bellah's narrative taken as a whole. In their essays, Paul Griffiths and Thomas Joseph White explain why that is so. But his anthropology of freedom is important and should be assimilated into a Christian anthropology. Christian theologians need to situate the biblical narrative in relation to the evolutionary narrative about the origins and ends of humanity. And I think that, to the extent that his anthropology puts creative freedom at the heart of human nature, Christian theologians can make use of Bellah's narrative.

Bellah, Robert. *Religion in Human Evolution: From the Paleolithic to the Axial Age.* Cambridge, MA: Harvard University Press, 2011.

Huizinga, Johan. *Homo Ludens: A Study of the Play Element in Culture.* New York: Beacon, 1955.

Plato, *The Laws.* Translated by Thomas L. Pangle. New York: Basic, 1980.

Ratzinger, Joseph. *Principles of Catholic Theology.* San Francisco: Ignatius, 1989.

12. Ibid., 89.

I.2 Impossible Pluralism

Paul Griffiths

ROBERT BELLAH UNDERSTANDS RELIGION as an activity that takes us beyond the quotidian. The everyday world is ordered by lack, of food, shelter,
sex, and so on; it is a world of demand and pressure and need. The non-
quotidian world is ordered by excess; it is a world of play and sleep and is
eventually given shape and made habitable by ritual, language, art, and so
on, with all their accompaniments and entails. In this non-quotidian world,
the fundamental mode of religious activity is ritual, and ritual serves as
deeply meaningful play. Play is the paradigmatic non-quotidian behavior.

Evolutionarily speaking, Bellah claims in his magnificent book *Religion in Human Evolution*, ritual-on-the-way-to-religion is an emergent
phenomenon, different in kind from what has gone before, in the same
(formal) way that life is a phenomenon emergent from the lifeless. Ritual
emerges in organisms—other mammals are ritualized beings, too, as are
birds—out of the matrix of play. Once it has emerged, religion follows
and becomes the principal generator of meaning and structure in human
societies.

The bulk of *Religion in Human Evolution* is devoted to analysis and
thickly described examples of how this has worked in particular cases, with
special attention paid to the emergence of theoretical cultures during the
Axial Age of the first millennium BC. The richly detailed chapters treating
tribal and archaic religion are thoroughly engaging. The synthesis of scholarship and many instances of nuanced historical judgment in long chapters
on ancient Israel, Greece, China, and India reflect an enviable intellectual
breadth and sympathy.

All that said, however, I have my doubts.

First, there's a question about whether the evidence at hand justifies the rich speculative sweep of the story Bellah tells. For example, at the beginning of his discussion of ancient Israel, he notes that there's "still only weak and contested consensus on such elementary facts as the dating of various biblical texts."[1] In his discussion of ancient Greece, he notes that it "is very hard to reconstruct social structure from archaeological data alone, and using Homer as a source of data is fraught with problems."[2] He also acknowledges disputes about the dating of texts, events, and ideas in ancient India.

Taken on their own, these areas of scholarly debate strongly suggest that we'll never know what really happened. This skeptical conclusion, Bellah says with disarming frankness, "is not an escape open to me."[3] That's because the requirements for a grand narrative of human history forbid it. "My comparative historical undertaking requires that I give some historical reality to the data or not use it at all."[4] When there isn't a scholarly consensus—which is most of the time—he promises to use his "common sociological sense of what is probable and what is not."[5] That's not reassuring, for "common sociological sense,"[6] I should think, is just shorthand for "a story I like the sound of."

Matters are worse yet with respect to human prehistory, about which we know almost nothing. We'd have more evidence relative to time span if we tried to reconstruct the 400-year sociocultural history of New York City from one worn shoe discarded in 1720 and a broken telephone dating from 1948. In this instance, as in the others, we should be very skeptical of the particulars of reconstructions based on such scanty evidence.

Such skepticism is supported by the realization that intellectual fashions change. More often than we're inclined to admit, scientific theories get revised, sometimes drastically. Almost no particular of the story I was taught forty-five years ago in respectable English schools about the evolution of the human species can now be found in high school or college textbooks that treat the subject. Few of the particulars of the four-source (J, E, D, P) hypothesis about the texts of the Pentateuch that I learned a little

1. Bellah, *Religion in Human Evolution*, 283.
2. Ibid.
3. Ibid.
4. Ibid.
5. Ibid., 284.
6. Ibid.

later as an assured result of modern scholarship now command the assent of anything more than a rump among contemporary biblical scholars. This is the usual thing: it would be easy to multiply examples.

What does this mean for a book of universal history like Bellah's? It means that we may be entertained, edified, or otherwise moved by its particulars but not instructed, at least not in the way that Bellah intends. It doesn't show us what happened—or if perchance it does, we haven't any reason to think that it does. What we have instead is a good and often edifying story. I don't see this as damning criticism. A vital intellectual culture needs grand narratives and large-scale explanatory myths, if you will. That's the only way we can integrate the particulars of scientific knowledge into an all-things-considered view of the way things are. But it's distressing that Bellah only occasionally sees with any clarity the nature of his project.

However unpersuasive about the past, *Religion in Human Evolution* reliably mirrors something of the present—the "common sociological sense" upon which Bellah so often relies. It's a principle of judgment best understood as a substantive view of what it means to be a flourishing human being. This brings me to my second concern: an under-warranted moralism.

That Bellah writes with moral purpose is clear. In his conclusion, he identifies two such purposes. He calls them "practical," but they are certainly also moral. First, he wants us to see that we human beings have evolved to a point where we have difficulty adapting to our adaptations. This may precipitate a "sixth great extinction event," an event in which vast numbers of species will be brought to extinction by us, with ourselves perhaps among their number. He writes that the hour is late, improvising on the end of 1 Corinthians 7. Second, in addition to preventing species disaster, he also wants us to abandon claims to the superiority of any one religious tradition over any or all others, a good he seems to think necessary for meeting the great ecological and social challenges of our time.

Exhortations to ecological concern and pleas for an end to claims of religious (and cultural) superiority are common in the subculture called academic, but their connection to the grand narrative of *Religion in Human Evolution* is obscure. Why, for example, is the hour late? I can easily imagine that someone coming to know that major extinction events are a regular feature of our planet's life, with or without human involvement, might think of them as like forest fires: perhaps necessary, even though prima facie destructive, and thus not necessarily to be prevented, even if they could be. This is my response to Bellah's story. Mass extinctions are part of the ordinary rhythm of life on this planet, it seems, as one might expect in a deeply damaged cosmos like ours (as it must axiomatically be said to be by Christian theologians).

Bellah's call for abandoning claims of religious superiority is even less convincing. He appears to think that taking seriously alien religious traditions in their own terms precludes, or at least sits uneasily with, judging one superior to another. But of course it doesn't: I can perfectly well appreciate, say, the precise technicalities of Sanskritic Buddhist scholasticism on their own terms, and judge that Catholic Christianity (my own tradition) might be instructed by them, without abandoning the claim that all salvation is mediated through Jesus Christ and that the Lord God established and maintains a relation with the people of Israel and with the church with a degree of intimacy given to no others.

So far as I can see—which may not be very far—nothing in the substance of Bellah's book supports the moral claims with which he ends it and that he takes it to serve. That is bad enough, perhaps, but there is much worse. His concluding words call for "the actualization of Kant's dream of a world civil society that could at last restrain the violence of state-organized societies toward each other and the environment."[7] This universalism, were it to be realized, would mean the end of the church (and, I think, of most other religious traditions, though I have neither the expertise nor the right to speak for them), as I will now go on to show.

Bellah's universal natural history of religion has many predecessors. David Hume, for example, in 1757 wrote a book called *The Natural History of Religion*, the professed goal of which was "to trace all [religion's] varied appearances, in the principles of human nature, whence they are derived."[8] Hume had a different understanding of religion than Bellah does, and he had a deeply different understanding of history, historiography, and human nature. Hume has somewhat different moral purposes as well: he wants to place kinds of religion in a hierarchy of better and worse, which Bellah explicitly disavows as a purpose or implication of his book.

So there are differences between Hume's enterprise and Bellah's. But the similarities are deeper and more revealing. Both want to diminish the tendency of religious people to think their own religion unsurpassable, and both adopt essentially the same method of doing this, which is to describe

7. Ibid., 606.
8. Hume, *Natural History of Religion*, 27.

Christianity (or Islam or Buddhism) as an emergent phenomenon, and to do so without using the vocabulary proper to it. The goal is to alter the modes of thought and modes of expression of Christians (and other religious people), to get them to think of their religious lives as a species of a genus rather than as sui generis.

Bellah doesn't want to be a reductionist and explicitly distances himself from sociobiological accounts of religion that can be seen as successors to Hume's approach. But in spite of these limitations, the religion that Bellah offers to Christians is transfigured every bit as much as that offered by Hume. To write a natural history of religion coupled with the hope that the history's lexicon and assumptions will replace those indigenous to particular religious traditions is to reproduce a Humean account, whether you like it or not.

And Bellah, disavowals notwithstanding, does like it. For it will be generic sociological and historical categories, not theological ones, that inform the self-understanding of the citizens of the hoped-for world civil society.

This desired future of the triumph of "common sociological sense" provides a hidden and important warrant for the grand narrative of *Religion in Human Evolution*. Kant's eschatology is found most pithily in his 1794 essay "Die Ende aller Dinge," which could well form an appendix to Bellah's book. In brief, Kant's eschatology is one of skepticism about our (human) capacity to understand or characterize the end of all things. Attempting to analyze and argue about the nature of human existence in eternity, or to determine who will be damned and who saved, exceeds reason's capacities.

This moralized eschatology dovetails with Bellah's. Kant thinks that advances in understanding (in this instance, of the true nature and purpose of eschatological thinking) ought to yield advances in good behavior. That is, if and only if you come to understand the exhaustively moral purpose of eschatological thought will you be improved by it. The curve of progress here is upward, even if asymptotic (a frequent Kantian point). Human beings approach the goal without finally reaching it.

There is, nevertheless, an upward curve, and movement along it is marked by moral improvement, increase in civility, and approach to "perpetual peace" (to mention the title of another of Kant's essays). Sages (Kant in his own view falls under this category), then, ought to be encouraged in their work of getting ordinary people (those who can't manage sagehood) to see that what the pious doctrines of religion are really about is the cultivation of practical reason, which is in any event the meaning and purpose of religion as he sees it.

Bellah is not Kantian in any technical sense, but he certainly shares Kant's assumptions about the meaning and purpose of religion and about the moral benefit of treatises like his own. Thus, there is a problem here whose face Bellah can see but that he tries to hold at arm's length. Humean natural histories and Kantian quasi-eschatologies typically, perhaps necessarily, place themselves at the apex of the conceptual and moral progress whose story they tell, and thereby inescapably place themselves as judges of what has come before. Bellah sees this and claims to avoid it. But he doesn't succeed.

Universal histories are by definition axiological—committed, that is, to an understanding of what is better and what is worse in the phenomena whose story they tell. Bellah's is no exception; his large-scale story has morals. Among them, perhaps central to them, is the thought that we (we humans? we Americans? we tenured professors who publish large books with university presses?) have no ground for triumphalism. His implicit (and, at the end, explicit) claim is that study of our long evolutionary past grounds, firmly, our conviction that triumphalism is no good.

The problem here is not that Bellah's universal history has an axiological axe to grind. The problem is incoherence. His anti-triumphalism is itself a triumphalism. Bellah is sure that he has taken what is good from Kant without Kant's racism; that he can see what is good in Mill's liberalism without Mill's approval of benevolent despotism; and that he is not guilty even of a speciesist triumphalism because he affirms the evolutionary advantages of bacteria and arthropods when compared to those of humans. But once it is remembered that most human beings have not had the advantage of Bellah's knowledge of the cosmos's long history, and that most have been, and most remain, triumphalist in just the sense that he finds undesirable, the triumphalism of his own universal history emerges into clear daylight. Most—nearly all—human beings have been deeply wrong and morally deformed by their triumphalism, which Bellah proposes to transcend and overcome.

There is in *Religion in Human Evolution* the sickly sweet scent of a self-righteousness blind to its own deformity. Bellah is no less triumphalist than Kant. He's just less aware of the nature of his triumphalism. Triumphalism, in just the sense that he understands it, is inextricable from the genre in which he writes. If you're doing Humean natural history and

Kantian eschatology—and it's not at all clear that a twenty-first-century academic writing a universal history with the categories and concepts of modern history and sociology can do otherwise—you will by definition be a triumphalist.

A universal history needs, as Bellah clearly sees, a metanarrative. That is, in order to be able to tell the story of everything, one must have a lexicon and syntax, which together constitute a grammar. The lexicon provides the nonnegotiable terms of art (they're always terms of art) by means of which the story is to be told, and the syntax provides the rules of combination in terms of which the lexicon is deployed. The grammar, the lexicon, and syntax in combination do not prescribe the particulars of the story, but they do determine the frame within which those particulars will be placed. Many different stories can be told with the same grammar, but they will all be the same kind of story (think of fairy stories, Whig histories, hard-boiled noirs, and so on).

In Bellah's case, the lexicon is a rich mix of the terms of art that belong to sociology of a stratospherically abstract kind with those that belong to evolutionary theory. Together, these provide his metanarrative, the narrative that, for him, frames and accounts for all other narratives, most especially those that belong to particular religious traditions. Moreover, he thinks it "the only shared metanarrative among educated people of all cultures that we have."[9]

Whether or not this is true depends, I suppose, on what's meant by "educated people"; I certainly do not share it, or at least not as a metanarrative, and I doubt that I am alone in this. That may be enough in Bellah's mind to exclude me, and those like me, from the set of educated people. But I think it would be more accurate to say that there is no universally shared metanarrative: not Bellah's, not Kant's, not that belonging to scholastic Buddhists, and not that belonging to orthodox Catholic Christians—to name only a few of the metanarratives available.

This is certainly true if we understand *metanarrative* as I've characterized it above, which is to say as a narrative that, in the eyes of its users, frames and explains all other narratives and can be framed and explained by none. To claim possession of a universally shared metanarrative is a hallmark of unreflective universal historians who would like to claim the conceptual and moral high ground by definitional fiat. Better to say that the metanarrative one has and offers is one candidate among many.

9. Bellah, *Religion in Human Evolution*, 600.

That's always the case, and I'll end these comments by sketching the one I have, and by attending especially to the place that Bellah's holds within it. For I do not take his narrative to be false (except when it becomes incoherent). It is, rather, preliminary and partial, because it fits into rather than frames and explains my own metanarrative, which I summarize as follows:

The cosmos—everything there is, save the Lord God, who is not a thing, or, if the term must be used, is *una summa quaedam res*—comes into being *cum tempore et cum spatiis*, i.e., with space-time as a central feature. This occurs by the free creative act of the Lord. It is not an event that can be dated or placed. The before-and-after of dating, and the here-and-there of placing, belong only to the cosmos, and to all of it without remainder; the cosmos therefore has no before and no outside. Every particular being in the cosmos is created ex nihilo by the Lord (all particular beings, therefore, are creatures) and has whatever being it has by way of participation in him.

Among these creatures are angels; (almost) simultaneously with creation (*in ictu*), some among these rebel against their creator and thereby introduce deep damage into the otherwise harmoniously beautiful space-time fabric of the cosmos. All creatures, material and immaterial, living and nonliving, are damaged by this fall. The Lord's response, indexed to time but not itself temporal, is to bring human beings, among many other kinds of creatures, into existence. (The evolutionary story that Bellah tells belongs here; its particulars occupy this place in the frame; and those particulars, as the framing narrative suggests, involve, without exception, death on a massive scale.)

Some among these creatures replicate the angelic fall, introducing new and worse damage into the fabric of the cosmos. The Lord's response (again, time-indexed but not itself temporal), a response whose *finis* is the transfiguring of the cosmos's chaotic deadly violence into an order more beautiful than the original, is to elect a person (Abraham) to special intimacy with himself, and to guarantee that same intimacy with his descendants. That response is intensified, eventually, by the Lord himself taking flesh, joining his substance with that of the man Jesus to become a single person, and in that flesh, as that person, dying and rising and ascending.

Human history then has the nexus of election and incarnation as its central thread; the fabric woven around this thread is of two colors, inextricably intertwined, one representing the love of the Lord, and the other the love of self, one peaceful and the other violent, one heavenly and the other hellish. (The particulars of Bellah's stories about specific human cultures belong here: They all have the people of Israel and the church as their vibrant center, whether proleptically or actually.)

Consequent upon the election and the incarnation is the gradual healing of the cosmos, which progresses principally through the work of the body of Jesus Christ—the church—here below, and culminates in an eschaton, an end whose particulars lie beyond the scope of this paragraph, and in which the two threads in the fabric are finally disentangled.

There's a metanarrative for you. Its grammar is that of Christian theology. It enframes Bellah's, fully accounting for it without rejecting any of its particulars that turn out to be true. This Christian metanarrative is of course not universally shared, understood, or offered, and in this it is just like Bellah's account. If his metanarrative is true, this Christian one must be false—because his account, he thinks, requires Christians exactly not to offer this narrative as a metanarrative. And if this Christian metanarrative is true, his must be false—not in its particulars, necessarily, but certainly in its self-understanding as a metanarrative. Metanarratives don't brook rivals.

I've learned a great deal from Robert Bellah's magnificent book. But what I've learned is about particulars: the ideas of facilitated variation and conserved core processes, for instance, and their possible purchase on the evolutionary process; and the sociological analyses given of particular human cultural forms. These can stand. But the metanarrative Bellah uses to frame them cannot. And since it's the metanarrative that gives the book its point, I'm left wondering what point remains when the metanarrative is seen for what it is.

Bellah, Robert. *Religion in Human Evolution: From the Paleolithic to the Axial Age.* Cambridge, MA: Harvard University Press, 2011.

Hume, David. *Dialogues and Natural History of Religion.* Oxford: Oxford University Press, 2008.

I.3 Sociology as Theology

Thomas Joseph White

JUST WHEN YOU THOUGHT liberal Protestantism was dead, Robert Bellah writes what is arguably the greatest work of liberal Protestant theology ever. *Religion in Human Evolution: From the Paleolithic to the Axial Age* is about the evolutionary roots of religious behavior. It is a magnificent treatment of ancient human religiosity, with particular focus on the civilizations of Israel, Greece, China, and India. The book begins with the Big Bang and terminates around two hundred years before Jesus of Nazareth, in the period that Karl Jaspers called the "Axial Age," the moment in history when human thought attained a genuinely universal character and a profound ethical maturity. In Bellah's magnum opus, which took thirteen years to write, he seeks to explain how we reached this axial age of universal reason and how religion helped us get there.

So why try to characterize it as a theology? The liberal Protestant tradition was concerned to defend the integrity and value of religion after the Enlightenment rejection of traditional Christianity. It insisted that we should no longer seek to defend religion by appeal to divine revelation and turned instead to the sociological role that religion plays in giving life a sense of ultimate purpose and in instilling ethical attitudes. Jesus teaches us what it means to be human and to love in an authentic way, and in that sense he brings the ethical project of humanity to its completion.

How could one credibly update such a vision today? In obvious ways, Bellah's work is quite different from that of Schleiermacher, Harnack, or Tillich: nowhere does he treat Jesus or Christianity, nor does he offer explicit theological or apologetic theses. Nonetheless, he does something Schleiermacher, Harnack, and Tillich never could. He sets their now-somewhat-dated vision of Christian humanism in successful dialogue with the two most important contemporary challenges to religious belief: evolutionary atheism and postmodern pluralism.

The former flatly denies any legitimate basis in human beings for religious behavior: why should a haphazard, randomly formed bundle of matter be religious? The latter asks why we should privilege Western, Christian canons of rationality and ethics over, say, those of ancient India. What Bellah does in both cases is genuinely intriguing—and theologically significant.

Bellah begins his treatment of evolution with the study of Big Bang cosmology, to which he adds astute sociological insights into the religious and the a-religious views of contemporary cosmologists. He then goes on to offer a detailed and eloquent portrait of the evolutionary origins of living things, from the single-celled prokaryotes and eukaryotes, the only living things for perhaps two billion years, to the development of complex mammals, progressing from chimpanzees to *homo erectus* and eventually to *homo sapiens*. Following biologists Marc Kirschner and John Gerhart, he suggests ways in which living things succeed more or less well owing to their new material adaptations. Consequently, it is the whole organism and not just its collection of genes that evolves through time. In natural selection, living things make use of their genetic alterations to engage their environment more successfully. We are not simply organic media through which genetic mutation makes its merry way.

This nonreductive vision of living beings provides an essential basis for Bellah's explanation of the emergence of advanced cognition in complex mammals. We are animals with adapted social features that permit us to pursue better forms of survival. Animals communicate to one another through mimicry, signaling, and even interactive play, and group membership becomes an advantage to the survival of the species. Bellah locates the remote origins of human culture in these communicative adaptations, especially in "play" as a "relaxed state" not ordered immediately toward either nutrition or procreation. Out of animal play come the capacities to mime, narrate, engage in ritual, and ultimately, theorize.

Such is the basis in human society for religion and philosophy, as well as modern science. We are still animals able to tell stories, even as our stories change over thousands of years, and even when we are narrating the history of the cosmos in a modern university lecture hall.

What is wrong with this picture? From a biological point of view, perhaps very little. What about from a religious point of view? For a Thomist, it does no harm to underscore the animal character of human thought and religiosity. By all means, invite the neuroscientists to measure every jot and tittle of brain activity present in a human being reciting the Nicene Creed. Aquinas himself affirms that rational animals always think conceptually through recourse to images and sense phantasms.

One would expect, then, corollary events in the cerebrum for every intellectual, spiritual act. Do we not pray on our knees or with our hands extended, or communicate meaning with the use of narrated stories and gestures? Only a Manichean would deny our embodied spiritual lives. Bellah has done a wonderful job of creating a space for profound conversation between biology and theology, in ways that are in fact implicitly consonant with the Catholic tradition.

The problem is that Bellah refuses the larger metaphysical questions that are always in the background of our modern cosmological storytelling. Our understanding of the cosmos and our biological development as animals have undergone an irreversible revolution: from Galileo to Newton to Darwin and Mendel. Bellah offers sharp and persuasive criticisms of reductive and materialist interpretations of this revolution. But in the end, the atheists who claim, often in the names of these indisputable scientific discoveries, to have resolved the meaning of life are reproposing something old-fashioned: the ancient metaphysics and ethics of Democritus and Lucretius, or even the views one might find in Buddhism or Parmenides—which is to say, new versions of materialism and Epicureanism, monism and compassionate nihilism. They are all formidable philosophical theories, but at the end of the day, they are also *just philosophical*.

Although Bellah's account of evolutionary science, culture, and religion is much more congenial to theological concerns, one needs to do more than criticize the philosophizing scientists for being unscientific. The perennial questions of classical philosophy must be addressed, and addressed in close connection with expansive scientific reflections of the sort Bellah offers. For example, it is certainly the case that the human frontal lobe, throat, tongue, and jawbone underwent an evolutionary development that made human speech and cognition possible. We find imperfect intimations of these developments in less sophisticated mammals, some of which are our ancestors.

But the passage from the linguistic sign to the conceptual universal and to intentional signification (reflexive thought) is another matter. It is one thing to be able to explain biologically how we are able to coordinate our bodily movement to dance to music we hear, but quite another to be able to explain what "justice" is. You can't reproduce justice by doing experiments on the frontal lobe, no matter how powerful the microscopes and electromagnetic impulses.

When human beings begin to think about the essences of things, or about what numbers or values are, or why the universe exists (which turns us toward the question of immaterial being), they do something that moves from the world of sensible singulars into the world of immaterial universals. Here the human *spiritual* animal acquires a new interiority alien to that of the other animals. Human beings rise up above the flux of nonrational beings. They judge their inner meaning and worth, as well as their ultimate causes.

Of course the materialists here will cry foul and claim that the study of neuroscience will inevitably allow us to explain away the residual belief in human "spiritual exceptionalism." The soul has got to go, along with fairies, ghosts, and God. Our evolutionary history will explain us "all the way down," exposing our intentional thought worlds and free decisions as hallucinations.

To which the right response is: no, actually. In fact, our human capacity to study our universe scientifically, including our neurological system and its evolution, is the product of our uniquely abstractive, spiritual capacity. And what is more, we *alone* among the animals can not only *understand* that history but also pass back behind it, as it were, to the deeper question of why the cosmos exists at all. We can look (as Aquinas does in the five ways) at the universe as a web of interconnected finite forms and interdependent causes and see that it is an inherently question-raising cosmos. Whence does all this come, and upon what (or whom) does it actually depend? As the only rational animal, we enjoy the privilege of asking the question of the existence of God.

Bellah rightly underscores the animality that undergirds all our intellectual, moral, and religious activities. But he does not engage the philosophical arguments that reflect on these same activities and that lead us to think about the immaterial soul, with its powers of intelligence and free will. There is a principle in the core of our being that comes from God directly and that is called to return to God. Consequently, it is the spiritual person as both body and soul who remains religiously restless and active in the material world. Each human being is a precarious bridge that runs between the visible world of matter and the invisible world of God.

Of course, Bellah will say that such thoughts outrun the limits of science and the disciplines of biology and sociology. That is quite true. But the excitement of reading *Religion in Human Evolution* stems in large part from the sheer ambition of the project—a genealogy of human culture that reaches toward universality. This quality leads Bellah to press beyond the narrow range of modern science. He is an academic pluralist who transgresses disciplinary boundaries. It is an indication of the deep taboos of our contemporary academic culture that the classical questions of metaphysics have no role to play in this book about the origins and purposes of all our religious beliefs, actions, and rituals.

Pluralism: what are we to make of the fact that there are many religions? Is there one true religion toward which all the others tend? Is there some one truth that gathers in all the other partial truths? St. Bonaventure, the medieval Franciscan theologian, seems to think so. Drawing on St. Augustine, he claims that the essence of religion consists in right worship: radical devotion of the heart offered to the true and living God. The prayer of Christ is such devotion offered perfectly, and Christ stands over history as the model of all religious and ethical endeavors. Other religions need not be rejected, then, as entirely false. Rather, the partial truths we find in them take on their ultimate value when they are purified by the illuminating light of Christ.

Hegel's *Lectures on the Philosophy of Religion* tells a secular version of this story. Christianity, for Hegel, is a religious precursor to the age of philosophical Enlightenment. Myth gives way to dogma and dogma to reason. Christianity itself eventually leads to secularization, and the perfection of secular reason is found not in Christ but in modern, democratic liberalism. In shorthand: the history of human culture begins in cave painting and finds its perfection in a globalized market economy, governed by the political principles of John Rawls.

Bellah wants to avoid both Bonaventure's and Hegel's triumphalist accounts and, for that matter, the triumphalism involved in any story of religious development that culminates in a single true religion or philosophy. Bellah insists that the pinnacles of civilization, the "breakthroughs" that make the Axial Age axial, are manifest in a diversity of cultures in different, nonreducible ways. Moreover, unlike Hegel and many other modern theorists, he insists that religious doctrines and rituals have enduring importance in sustaining culture. They are not merely a prehistoric skin that modern reason needs to eventually shed.

1.3 Sociology as Theology

This commitment to the enduring, nonreducible integrity of the different "axial breakthroughs"[1] is elaborated in the treatment of four archaic civilizations between the years 1200 and 200 BC. Bellah spends almost 350 pages on ancient Israel, Greece, China, and India. In each case, he seeks to show that the archaic religions of the past established a framework from which universal, critical thinking emerged.

For example, ancient Greek religious rituals and Homeric legends provided a cradle for the development of civic democracy. The religious practice of ancient theater—Aeschylus and Euripides were originally performed in a liturgical context—created a symbolic form of reflection on human existence, which prepared the way for ancient philosophy (particularly that of Plato and Aristotle). Similarly, the ancient ethical reflections of the Hebrew prophets gave rise to normative legal theories about the meaning of the state and its obligations and its limitations in the face of human dignity. Confucian and Daoist theorists debated the relative importance of the political community with respect to the larger natural order and the environment. In India, as Bellah notes, the criticisms of Brahman culture made by the Buddha led to egalitarian ethical reforms within Brahmanism itself.

This commitment to pluralism distinguishes Bellah from his liberal Protestant forebears. Their theologies were organized around philosophical anthropology, a general theory of man as a religious animal. But in substantive and sometimes covert ways, they retained a christological center or end point. The fully religious and human way of living invariably ended up taking a Christian form, however remotely.

Unlike Schleiermacher and Hegel, Bellah wants to avoid the promotion of a uniquely Christian vision of the religious essence of man. He is weary of a cheap religious syncretism that ignores the real differences of belief and practice among the ancient religions. In the end, then, he decides for the multicultural option: the essence of human religion is not identified comprehensively by any one tradition but is refracted to us through a multiplicity of traditions. Each offers partially convergent, partially incompatible visions of the meaning of reality. The search for a universal ethics characterizes them all. Each of the axial religious traditions narrates after its own fashion a social life governed by moral norms. But we cannot distill an essence. The universality of the Axial Age cannot be separated from the particularity of its religious embodiments.

1. Bellah, *Religion in Human Evolution*, 279.

The diversity among religions should not lead us to despair, his analysis suggests, but to study and conversation. Our public culture should provide space for respectful religious inquiry and discussion. Something like "religious studies," conducted with a spirit of intensive immersion in the thought world of religious traditions, needs to revitalize our religious imaginations. Bellah finishes his sprawling narrative of ancient human religiosity with an appeal to Immanuel Kant's ethics of universal peace.

Here again this seemingly untheological book is theologically resonant. Bellah's proposal is emblematic of both the nobility and the inner agony of the liberal Protestant tradition. Its nobility stems from its catholic aspiration to universal knowledge. What is the "natural law" inherent to all human, religious cultures? Why does man incessantly search for the absolute? How does the study of cosmology, evolutionary theory, and the history of religions either challenge or promote a broader understanding of this religious dimension of the human person? When we ask such questions, no legitimate claimant to the truth should be ignored.

No truth except that of divine revelation, as well as metaphysics, the mode of reflection that the church long ago recognized as the intellectual handmaiden for a theology that speaks about God. And herein lies the hidden misery of liberal Protestantism, built in from the start. The price for admission to the Enlightenment university club was the agreement to check at the door all appeals to dogmatic, supernatural revelation. Religion without revelation. The problem with this is it's not rational.

Consider that human history exhibits a fascinating range of religious behaviors and beliefs but that the same complexity invites us naturally to inquire after the absolute truth. What, in the end, is the case regarding the nature of reality and the truth of religion? To a certain degree, Bellah offers his own covert answer. In his concluding remarks, readers begin to sense that he regards the capacity for critical reflection and prophetic witness as the deep truth about religion, and it's the university and its academic culture that now nurture this genius.

Consider further that the interminable confusion and complexity of human religious behavior suggests another idea, one of equal consequence: that by our own powers we cannot finally resolve all the questions. The meaning of human religiosity remains enigmatic. Then can we not rightfully ask: What if God has revealed himself to humanity? If God has revealed himself, Christ and the biblical covenant are the lights that ultimately govern the nations, inviting all real but partial truths into a deeper unity, one purified from the dregs of human ignorance and error. In this case, divine revelation is not the enemy of human reason but is the intelligent answer given to the many ages of human religious question-asking. Final truth speaks to something deep within us but is itself a gift, not something conquered by the unique lights of human investigation.

What, then, is our human religiosity? It is a sign of our latent desire for the truth about God, but it is also a sign of our confusion and fallenness. Religion without grace remains precarious—and even pernicious. Bellah underscores the prevalence of human sacrifice in a diversity of ancient religions, East and West: obscure sacrifices made to obscure powers. The life of grace, meanwhile, is something distinct from the religious acts of our fallen humanity even when it is acting at its best.

Contrary to the thinking of liberal Protestantism, which sought to build theology only from the bottom up, true religion is established not through the evolution of human culture but by the charity of the God-man and the infusion of his grace. Contrary to the thinking of Barth, however, human religion is not abolished in Christ and his members. Rather, it is healed, purified, and elevated by divine charity. The fragments of a true human religiosity previously refracted in the various religious traditions of man are regathered in a new form, illumined from within by the light of Christ.

Religions don't just come to be, develop, and evolve. They also die. Bellah gives many examples of religious cultures that came and went throughout antiquity. Many of the greatest representatives of these religions arose, as he notes, at times of crisis, when their traditions were on the verge of extinction. Ironically, Bellah himself may be an instance of this phenomenon. For, like Hegel, he has offered a profound master narrative of human history, one that shows the power of modern Protestant intellectual life and of the university culture that it inspired. But unlike Hegel, Bellah writes at a time after the decline and eclipse of mainline Protestant culture and its quest for an Enlightenment universalism that made room for faith. If religion is evolving in the world today, it does not seem to be headed in his direction.

Traditional Christians should mourn the loss of such compelling interlocutors, especially in a post-Christian world where religious literacy wanes. Barth reacted to the cosmopolitan aspirations of liberal Protestantism with a cosmopolitan dogmatism of his own. The *Church Dogmatics* is a vast attempt to talk about virtually everything from a christocentric point of view. In one sense, Barth was unquestionably correct: Without commitments to christological absolutes, Christianity folds, and it is those absolutes that give us ultimate perspective.

At the same time, a dogmatic religion, even if entirely true, should give an account of itself in the public square, speaking to public reason. This entails not only proclamation but also explanation. How does the revelation of Christ relate to natural reason in the domains of modern science, philosophy, ethics, and the history of religion? Bellah challenges us to consider our answers to these questions in profound ways. He also provides us with a great deal of historical material to think about toward this end.

Christians should be willing to learn from both Barth and Bellah as we move forward in the evolution—or, better yet, organic development—of a unified, Christian view of reality. Doing so will require the continuation of dogmatic thinking that is distasteful to our post-Enlightenment neighbors who can see in dogma nothing but dogmatism. But it also requires that theology engage deeply the modern sciences and that it process in a critical way the intellectual, moral, and religious patrimony of human culture, whether it is Eastern or Western, archaic or modern, secular or religious.

The catholic aspiration to seek the truth underlying all things is not utopian. In a real sense, the fullness of the Truth has already become manifest: the Wisdom who became flesh and dwelt among us. The revelation of Christ is a shock to our myopic religious leanings, as well as to our provincial secularism. He speaks to what is best in us, which is often hidden from our own eyes. He also challenges and reproves what is old and outdated, tearing down our idols and letting in new light.

Even if it lacked the fullness of proclamation, here the liberal Protestant tradition was right, and Robert Bellah's ambitious universal history of humanity can provide a proper theological inspiration. He who was crucified and who rose from the dead, the Alpha and Omega of the human race, fulfills and perfects our native religiosity. Working in the light of his grace, our religious cultures can become simultaneously human and divine, evolved from the basic conditions of biological life and a supernatural gift. In Christ we can acknowledge rightfully the union of revelation and reason, grace and nature, God and man. This too is "evolution," though one of a radically new sort. It is the beginning of a new life, the inevitable future of all true human religion.

Bellah, Robert. *Religion in Human Evolution: From the Paleolithic to the Axial Age.* Cambridge, MA: Harvard University Press, 2011.

I.4 A Reply to My Critics

Robert Bellah

PERHAPS IT WAS INEVITABLE in a symposium organized by *First Things* that all three commentators fault my book for not taking the life, death, and resurrection of Jesus Christ as the center of my story, when the fact of the matter is that my book didn't reach chronologically to the life of Jesus. That's because *Religion in Human Evolution*, large as it is, is a fragment. I had originally intended to bring the book up to the present, but when in 2010 the manuscript had become so tall that it could almost tip over I realized that it must go to the publisher with the hope for another (inevitably smaller) book to complete what I had originally hoped to do. I rationalized this decision on the grounds that it did achieve, I hoped, one major point that was central to my argument: by looking at where religion came from rather than where it was going, I could avoid what I thought were the major defects of most previous efforts to account for the evolution of religion—namely, determinism and reductionism.

It was precisely in an attempt to defeat efforts to reduce religion to deterministic and reductionist biological causes that I undertook at my advanced age a fairly serious education in biology so that I could show that those accounts could not be substantiated in biological terms. I was then also concerned to avoid sociological or economic determinism by showing instead that religion, from the earliest forms to the great transformations of the Axial Age, had its own inner dynamic and creativity, which made it impossible to treat it as a "variable" determined by its social environment, however much it interacted with and responded to that environment.

So I wish my critics had focused more on what I did do than on what I didn't do. But under the circumstances, that was understandable. Theologians will be theologians, I suppose.

Francesca Aran Murphy, in her emphasis on freedom, comes closest to getting at what I was most trying to do in this book, and her criticisms are off the mark by only a little. She and I share a great admiration for Johan Huizinga's *Homo Ludens*, which has been central in both of our lives. However, she sees Huizinga following Plato when he, in the *Laws*, wrote that "man is made God's plaything, and that is the best part of him,"[1] but she does not see me doing so. Why does she imagine that I don't affirm Plato as Huizinga does? Nothing in what follows the Plato quote in *Religion in Human Evolution* indicates any disavowal on my part. And the fairly long and largely ecstatic treatment of Plato in the chapter on Greece in the Axial Age would certainly suggest to most readers that I am a Platonist.

She comes to her conclusion in part because elsewhere in the book I quote Kant with approval and so must believe, as she thinks Kant does, that freedom is purely negative, freedom *from*, rather than freedom *for* the fulfillment of our natures. But of course, Kant specifically thinks of the freedom at the basis of the categorical imperative as *positive*—that is, the freedom to treat oneself and all others as ends in themselves, thus producing a "kingdom of ends," which is the ideal society. Plato and Kant arrive at their conclusions in very different ways, but both see freedom as for something.

After largely agreeing with my argument, Murphy writes, "It is quite impossible for an orthodox Christian theologian to buy into Bellah's narrative taken as a whole."

That raises the question of what "Bellah's narrative as a whole" really is, something that bedevils all the contributions to the symposium (and preoccupied much of the discussion at the seminar last December as well). But for now, let's leave aside "my narrative" and take up the issue of what is and isn't possible for orthodox Christians. Murphy is attentive to my references to Huizinga and then to Plato, yet she ignores my reference to Blaise Pascal, who makes a rather surprising appearance in a chapter on my very lukewarm account of "religious naturalism." There I quote him affirming not the God of the philosophers but God incarnate in Jesus Christ. Perhaps Pascal appears where he does to make a point not entirely incompatible with "orthodox Christian theology."

While I am honored by Thomas Joseph White's assertion that *Religion in Human Evolution* is "the greatest work of liberal Protestant theology ever," I nonetheless would like to decline the honor. I wrote my book as an example of one possible kind of contemporary social science, interdisciplinary

---

1. Plato, *Laws*, 796.

even to the point of including natural science along with social sciences and the humanities. Still, I believe that all our categories overlap, and so my book does not require excluding revelation and metaphysics but is, on the contrary, open to them in a variety of ways. A book can address topics of theological import without being a book of theology.

That said, it is probably "liberal Protestant" that gives me more trouble than "theology." I consider Paul Tillich one of my three great teachers. I know he is often categorized as a liberal Protestant, but he doesn't fit. He was a critic not only of liberal Protestantism (for just the reason White cites: it had liquidated itself into secular humanism) but also of Protestantism itself. His book *The Protestant Era* was first proposed as *The End of the Protestant Era?*, but his publisher didn't want a question mark in the title; he then titled it *The End of the Protestant Era*, but Protestant friends felt that seemed to suggest he was becoming Catholic, so he ended up with the title we know.

Tillich's criticism of Protestantism itself, which was very deep and led to his feeling that he lived at the end of "the Protestant era," was based on his understanding of Christianity. He consistently affirmed "the Protestant principle," which is in essence prophetic religion that calls everything on this earth into question relative to a transcendent conception of God. However, the Protestant principle also requires what he called "Catholic substance," in the absence of which the Protestant principle turns into sheer criticism, which finally turns on itself and becomes nihilistic. For Tillich, the essence of Catholic substance is sacramentalism, and it is exactly that which Protestantism abandoned. First, orthodox Protestantism proclaimed the Word and the Sacrament; then it became the Sacrament through the Word; and then it became just the Word. For example, when Karl Barth said the Word of God did not contain the sentence "Thou shalt light candles," he made Tillich's point. Even more crushing was Tillich's claim that Protestant theology had abandoned love as the central theological virtue in place of the all-consuming emphasis on faith.

For me, accepting Tillich's criticism of liberal Protestantism, and of Protestantism itself (though not the Protestant principle), meant that I could only be a small-*p* protestant. Through my decades of involvement in the Berkeley Graduate Theological Union, where I was an adjunct professor from the time I first came to Berkeley in 1967, and especially owing to my close collaboration with faculty and graduate students at the Jesuit School of the GTU, I lived in a heavily Catholic atmosphere even in so secular a place as Berkeley. Though I had been raised as a Presbyterian I ended up an Episcopalian, where liturgy and the Eucharist in particular met my need for a sacramental religious practice. So I ended up a small-c catholic (or Anglo-Catholic) as well as a small-p protestant. For all these reasons, I don't want to be called a liberal Protestant theologian, however great.

To the extent that I'll accept the honor of being called a theologian, it's along the lines of what Tillich himself described in a talk to the Harvard Overseers of 1959. He said that all academic study in the humanities, and especially in religion, must combine detachment or distance with participation. In the empirical cases I treat in my book, revelation and metaphysics are not parked at the door.

On the contrary, several have significant existential meaning to me. "Nothing is ever lost" became my mantra. In the case studies of my book I sought the passion of participation that Tillich rightly recognized must complement detached analysis. My treatment of the biblical Hebrew prophets in my chapter on ancient Israel takes me back to my high school church experience, when I first read them and where they indelibly formed in me a social Christianity that I have never abandoned. I especially identify with Jeremiah, with his terrible burden of being called by God, though he dearly wished God had chosen someone else. Through much of my adult life I have been reading Plato and Aristotle, Aristotle long before I read *After Virtue*, but with increasing understanding after that. I first read Confucius and Mencius in classical Chinese in my first year in graduate school, where I was combining a degree in sociology with East Asian languages. They have never left me. In my research on ancient India, where I was completely a novice, I met the Buddha of the Pali Canon for the first time, despite my long familiarity with Mahayana Buddhism in East Asia, where the "historical Buddha" is completely overshadowed by the Bodhisattvas. I was entranced with what I found: such wonderful, wise, and often amusing dialogues. Even in the chapter on tribal religion, I noted how much the Australian Aborigines, especially as described by the Australian anthropologist W. E. H. Stanner, and the Navajo, as described by my own undergraduate teachers at Harvard, have meant to me.

So I don't entirely deny that there is theology in my book—indeed, what would it be if there weren't? And perhaps White will insist that I'm being too ingenious in my use of Tillich to parry the liberal Protestant label. I'm willing to concede that it's the theologian's prerogative to define theological categories. But I'd like to challenge White's sociological assumptions about theological traditions.

He notes the irony of my remarkable achievement of a liberal Protestant theology just at the moment when liberal Protestantism is in eclipse. I think that is more of an open question than he does. The "eclipse" may be due to the triumph of liberal Protestantism. By so invading secular humanist culture that it lost its own distinction, it won, after all, by transforming secular humanist culture itself. There is more than a little evidence that most Americans, for example, would assent to unmarked liberal Protestant beliefs more often than to unmarked orthodox alternatives, and that this would be true not only for most mainline Protestants but also for most Catholics and even most Evangelicals.

I joked in our seminar that liberal Protestantism had died and been reborn; it is called "religious studies." Religious studies is not a homogeneous field, but I think there is more than a little truth in what I said, and that the replacement of theology departments with religious studies departments in most American universities (and now in Europe and Asia too) is a sign that liberal Protestantism as White envisages it is alive and well, being taught to tens of thousands of students every year.

There are other signs of triumph. Many have noted the process of "Protestantization" of the "world religions" (the very term is a liberal Protestant invention). Reform movements in Hinduism, Buddhism, Confucianism, even Islam, with Reform Judaism being a vivid example, all exhibit this process. Some have seen Vatican II in this light. It may seem that radical fundamentalism has won the day, but in sheer numbers the fundamentalists are probably eclipsed in most traditions by liberal reformist alternatives, who are quieter but more numerous. The emergence of a vigorous human rights agenda in global civil society is another partial offshoot of liberal Protestantism. And what the growing number of religious "nones" in America believe is far less likely to be atheism than some residual form of unorganized liberal Protestantism. One can find liberal Protestantism inadequate, though not without redeeming qualities, as I do, without presuming it is near death.

Paul Griffiths has some nice things to say about *Religion in Human Evolution*, but he soon begins the process of demolishing my book by questioning its entire substance on two grounds. First, he believes there is not enough evidence for such a story. At moments, it seems Griffiths is so skeptical about the adequacy of our knowledge of the things I try to cover in my book that he thinks no one could ever write a coherent account. Second, he claims I use what evidence there is willfully to suit myself. He argues that I am arbitrary, that I am telling "a story I like the sound of."

Here, all I can say in my defense against the first criticism is that I did the best I could. Like any scholarly book, certainly any history book, it will be quickly outmoded in its details because of new scholarship. But in the thirteen years I worked on my book, I sought the most reliable accounts I could find. My book is deeply collaborative. I consulted not only basic texts where they were available (relying mainly on translations, though with key texts in more than one translation), but also on the classic secondary literature, as well as on the state-of-the-art secondary literature at the time of writing.

In many cases I consulted specialists, some of whom are at Berkeley but most of whom are scattered all over the world. (I have my doubts about modern information technology, but I have to say I could not have written this book without email.) I sought and largely obtained readings that told me where I was wrong and helped me to get things right, or at least defensible, in area after area where I was not a specialist or, in the case of India, had no background at all.

If Griffiths wants to believe there is no objective basis for the stories I tell, he can of course do so. But I'm less of a skeptic. Scholars sometimes have to venture synthetic judgments, especially if we want to have something informed to say about large-scale questions of the sort I try to answer, however tentatively, however fallibly, in my book.

His second criticism turns on what I can only describe as a monomaniacal approach to metanarratives. He believes a metanarrative is "a narrative that, in the eyes of its users, frames and explains all other narratives and can be framed and explained by none." When I take up the discussion of metanarratives in my second chapter (I have to wonder if he even read that chapter) I outline an entirely different view. I am concerned with many metanarratives and indicate that none of them can subsume all the others. For example, I say that "there is one story about origins that, at least among educated people, has a kind of priority today, and that is the story as told by science: in terms of the universe, scientific cosmology; in terms of life, evolution." I go on to say that, although this is a story I can't avoid, "that does not mean it is the only story. In the course of writing this book, which is a history of histories, and story of stories, I have become involved with many of the stories I recount to the point of at least partial conversion."

In other words, although I take the scientific story as a necessary framework, I reject it as an adequate religious myth, though some people have proposed to do so. For example, the astute reader will note that Teilhard de Chardin, a favorite of those who want to fuse science with religion, is not mentioned once in my book. I engage in critical exegesis of such efforts and show what is wrong with their approach. Thus, if Griffiths had read carefully, he would know that the scientific story is to me only a convenience for exposition and not *my* myth. I call the religious interpretation of the scientific story of cosmology and biological evolution a "myth" not in a pejorative sense but to indicate that using that story for religious purposes has moved out of the realm of science.

I attempt to reclaim the use of the term *myth* that allows for pluralism, rather than the monism Griffiths presupposes, when I write:

> Myth can be true, but it is a different kind of truth from the truth of science and must be judged by different criteria. . . . I would argue that the myths told by the ancient Israelite prophets, by Socrates, Plato, and Aristotle, by Confucius and Mencius, and by the Buddha, just to stay within the purview of this book, are all true myths. They overlap with each other and with [the scientific myth], but even in their conflicts, which are sometimes serious, they are all worthy of belief, and I find it possible to believe in all of them in rather deep but not exclusive ways.

I know that this opens me to the charge of relativism from Griffiths (with which I will deal later), but it shows decisively that I have no mono-myth designed to replace all others. I criticize and disavow the use of the modern cosmological and evolutionary myth as an adequate religious story, and I certainly do not use it as "my story." To the extent that Griffiths thinks that I do, and Murphy and White seem to indicate that they agree, they have all failed to read carefully enough. So when Murphy writes that as "an orthodox Christian theologian" she "cannot buy into Bellah's narrative taken as a whole," I wonder what narrative she is talking about. It is not my conscious intent to offer such a narrative.

When I move beyond biology to the realm of culture, I am leaving behind the scientific narrative that "all educated people accept." I am developing insights from Merlin Donald, Jerome Bruner, and others to try to understand aspects of cultural evolution. Here I move into contested territory, since some scholars think that the idea of evolution applies only to biology and not to culture, and others believe that cultural evolution is defensible but have a different view from the one I adopted. I'm fully aware of the lack of scientific consensus on these issues. Still further, I am not so foolish as to imagine that the two issues I raise at the end of my conclusion—namely, the danger of ecological catastrophe and the necessity of sympathetic understanding of all human traditions—command anything like universal agreement. Here I am doing exactly what Griffiths thinks I should be doing: agreeing that "the metanarrative one has is one candidate among many." I am not offering one more triumphalist metanarrative.

I find the charge bizarre. Triumphalist narratives usually offer a final stage that is a "fulfillment" of all previous stages. Yet the few hints I give about where the story I tell seems to be headed lead to exactly the opposite conclusion. I have profound doubts about the modern project itself, which has significant achievements but seems headed toward self-destruction. I argue that the theoretic, which modern culture tends to exalt, is not the final culminating stage that can dispense with everything before it. Yes, it is powerful in some ways compared with its predecessors, the mimetic and the mythic, but it is also vulnerable to great dangers precisely when it becomes disembedded from bodily practice and narrative.

Thus, when it comes to religion understood as "a conception of a general order of existence,"[2] as Clifford Geertz puts it, I prefer Plato's to that of modern science used as a religious myth. In fact, I think all the axial myths are preferable to that latter alternative. I believe in multiple metanarratives, in many histories and many stories, and therefore I cannot accurately be accused of asserting a single triumphalist story, and especially not the one modern science has on offer. "Metanarratives don't brook rivals," Griffiths writes. His might not, but I find that claim a theoretical abstraction. As I show, during the Axial Age, world history *did* offer rivals—and it still does. One of the major points of my book is that we should avoid using a triumphalist scientific metanarrative by subsuming or resolving or domesticating this rivalry.

Griffiths takes up two positions that I find profoundly shocking. One is his casual acceptance of a future of mass extinction for humans and probably most multicellular life. He writes that "major extinction events are a regular feature of our planet's life, with or without human involvement." Here he is simply wrong. All previous extinction events have been caused by physical occurrences such as collisions with comets or meteorites or massive volcanic eruptions. Only this one is caused by humans, and only this

2. Geertz, *Interpretation of Cultures*, 90.

one can humans do something about. I thought Catholics were especially concerned about life. How can Griffiths be so complacent about passively accepting the death of millions, or billions, or very possibly all human lives?

I have recently reread *Gaudium et Spes* and noted that, while it warns us against the illusion that flawed human beings can bring about the kingdom of God on earth, we are not to use that as an excuse to not do all we can to bring our present world as close as possible to that end. Human weakness is rejected as an excuse for inaction in the face of worldly evils. I am certain that humans can still do a lot to mitigate the environmental disasters already beginning (how often in history has lower Manhattan been underwater?) but am not optimistic that we will act effectively in time. In this case, Kant's "can" surely means "should," and I can't imagine Griffiths's complacency in so serious a matter.

The other thing that shocked me was Griffiths' horror at the idea of a world civil society, which he believes "would mean the end of the church and, I think, of most other religious traditions." Why on earth would he think that a global civil society would mean the end of the church? History suggests otherwise. Freedom of religion is the very first commitment of civil society, going back to its origins in the eighteenth century. All the other freedoms that civil society requires, such as freedom of speech, of the press, of association, and so forth, are extrapolations from that one central freedom, the freedom of religion. For a long time the Catholic Church supported the idea of an established church and was doubtful about religious freedom, but several of the central documents of Vatican II indicate a strong affirmation of religious freedom. A world civil society of the sort I hope (as does a major strand of modern Catholicism) will flourish is therefore more likely to mean an end to religious persecution than the end of religion.

Jürgen Habermas and others also support the idea of a global civil society. We have a global economy that transcends and intimidates all nations, but we have nothing above the nation-state to mitigate the dangers of the unconstrained use of national power, even for genocide. Further, nationalism is one of the greatest dangers in our world today, especially since the two most powerful nations in the world, the United States and China, are its two most nationalist. The idea of a war between China and the United States is not inconceivable as things are going at the moment, but that would be disastrous and could lead to the same consequences as environmental disaster.

In any event, a global civil society open to pluralism is already beginning to show its head. I was in China twice in 2011 and saw the hope young intellectuals there had that such a development could mitigate the authoritarianism of their own country and lead to a genuine engagement of China with the other leading nations of the earth. These young Chinese wanted a civil society with no state ideology—not Marxism, not Confucianism—but rather the open discussion of all the alternatives, in which a chastened Confucianism would have a voice, though only in dialogue with the traditional religions of Buddhism and Daoism, as well as with Christianity, a growing religion in China and the faith, as these young intellectuals well knew, of many Chinese dissidents.

Whether it is an all-consuming "metanarrative" or the supposed anti-Christian consequences of a world civil society, Griffiths consistently suspects that I am offering some kind of mono-myth that would swallow up everything else: "If Bellah's metanarrative is true, this Christian one must be false—because his account requires Christians exactly not to offer this narrative as a metanarrative." The nonrelativistic pluralism that I espouse is simply incomprehensible to him, as it was to many of the symposium participants. When I recite the Nicene Creed in church I think I am asserting a metanarrative not so far from his, although he can't imagine that I could seriously believe it. But I do. I wrote *Religion in Human Evolution* not as a narrow professional undertaking but as a work of social science that I value existentially, because it tries to bring into clearer focus what role religion has in the development and flourishing of the human animal. And I've studied Navajo religion, which evokes in me insights I cherish rather than a demand that I reject it as a competing "metanarrative."

As I read Griffiths's commentary, I have to wonder, has he really read my book? The last thing I am arguing for is "generic sociological and historical categories, not theological ones, that [will] inform the self-understanding of the citizens of the hoped-for world civil society." What I believe is exactly the opposite, as I affirm in the crucial quotation from Thomas McCarthy, Habermas's leading American interpreter, in the penultimate paragraph of my book: "The conceptual point is this: *By their very nature, the universal cannot be actual without the particular, nor the formal without the substantive, the abstract without the concrete, structure without content.*"[3]

---

3. McCarthy, *Race, Empire, and the Idea of Human Development*, 187.

And so it follows that "from our present perspective, it is clear that the irreducible variety of hermeneutic standpoints and practical orientations informing interpretive endeavors, however well informed, will typically issue in a 'conflict of interpretations' and thus call for a dialogue across differences."[4] Our religious convictions will make vital contributions to any world civil society that is fit for actual human beings.

Griffiths finally finds my book pointless. Thankfully, the other commentators to some degree seem to think that I succeeded in fulfilling the two goals I set for myself. First, a serious look at the present state of work in evolutionary biology shows that it by no means requires an absolutely determinist and reductionist view. Many leading biologists recognize the sentience, creativity, and participation of organisms in their own evolution as being there from the beginning and believe that genetic mutation is only one part of the story, not its absolute foundation. Conserved core processes are able to defend themselves from genetic changes that would destroy them, while encouraging changes that might enhance them. For these and other related reasons, attempts to use biology to explain culture need not have grim reductionist consequences. We're spiritual by nature, as it were.

Second, in my chapters beginning with tribal religion right up to the Axial Age, I argue that religion involves a quest for comprehensive meaning that has its own internal motivation. It occurs within and interacts with other spheres of society and culture, but what it produces can never be reduced to those environing spheres. I reject the older, often taken-for-granted economic determinism in the long story I tell, and I also reject the newer turn to power determinism that is so popular among the postmodernists. Thus, in terms of both biological and cultural history, I argue for freedom and creativity rather than determinism and reductionism. This is surely of some help to those students of religion who already intuit that to be the case, as Murphy suggests most of us do.

Beyond that, I take every case on its own terms, affirming revelation and metaphysics where I find them, and also the claim to the truth of their own metanarratives, which can never be subsumed into "my metanarrative." I believe there is truth in all of them, including the tribal ones. All of them deserve our respect. That does not mean all of them are to be believed as equally true, which I have never affirmed. But it does mean we can learn from all of them.

---

4. Bellah, *Religion in Human Evolution*, 606.

Bellah, Robert. *Religion in Human Evolution: From the Paleolithic to the Axial Age.* Cambridge, MA: Harvard University Press, 2011.

Geertz, Clifford. In *The Interpretation of Cultures.* New York: Basic, 1973.

McCarthy, Thomas. *Race, Empire, and the Idea of Human Development.* Cambridge: Cambridge University Press, 2009.

Plato. *The Laws.* Translated by Thomas L. Pangle. New York: Basic, 1980.

I.5 Ritual and Religion

Lenn Goodman

THEORISTS AT LEAST SINCE Darwin have sought functional explanations for the ubiquity of religion. Unwilling to accept Stoic arguments *ex consensu gentium* that pursue an objective correlative of human spiritual yearnings, but loath to dismiss religion as a mere category error or bastard offspring of ignorance and fear, evolutionists have long sought some utility in religion, perhaps in the past, or even (since religions do persist), *for someone* in the present. In *Religion in Human Evolution*, Robert Bellah gathers years of work into an expanding meditation on this subject—though perhaps not with greater success than the theorists before him. One postulate of his approach is Lamarckian: human history is evolution by other means; cultural evolution is its engine. Bellah grounds his functionalist hypothesis in ritual, a broader realm than religion and responsive to multiple needs. Taking up a thought from Mihaly Csikszentmihalyi, Bellah understands ritual in terms of *flow*, "a kind of optimal experience of full engagement with the world and full engagement of one's own potentialities."[1] Zen practices are prime examples. So are Sabbaths. Such rituals ease life's anxieties. Evolution tells the story: ritual evolves from play. Csikszentmihalyi finds paradigm cases of flow among "ordinary Americans at work." But that, Bellah suggests, must reflect a shift of work toward ritual. Work, as such, is something of a curse. The constancies of daily life make it ultimately unbearable, "a world of lack," bearing "no guaranteed success." Play, like sleep and dreaming, is more than a respite then. It becomes redemptive. Ritual, in functional terms, does the work of play.[2]

1. Bellah, *Religion in Human Evolution*, 10.
2. Ibid., 9–10.

Play, Bellah argues, reflects relaxed selection pressures. Anchored in rules of moral equality, play opens doorways to ritual and art. The description is self-validating: when animal play turns too rough and deference to the weaker is forgotten, play lapses into struggle with its demand (or consequence) of hierarchy. Likewise in ritual: agrarian and urban life displace egalitarian rules with "a dominance unknown to hunter gatherers."[3] There's ritual and ritual, then; play and play.

In Aztec ballgames, spectators on the winning side chased down their opponents and stripped them of their jewelry. In an annual twenty-one-day festival, warriors acting the part of Xipe Totec, the god of gladiatorial combat, "wore the flayed skins of sacrificed war captives until they rotted off."[4] (One might be forgiven for failing to quite see the joyous optimal engagement of flow.) But on Bellah's account, if there's a problem here it lies not in play or ritual per se but in the intrusion of hierarchy and hegemony. The axiology Bellah builds into his evolutionary scheme commends a return to easier ways: play at its purest, Bellah finds among tribal communities and animals.

Here, his argument begins to falter. The relaxation of selection pressures in animal play is controversial at best. Granted, as far as anyone can tell, well-fed orcas *enjoy* tossing baby seals about before releasing their traumatized victims, just as a cat toys with a mouse, and kittens tussle with each other. It's hardly clear that these carnivores are not merely sharpening their hunting skills, learning moves too subtle to master without practice.

Bellah admiringly quotes Schiller's description of a lion's "high-spirited roaring" as "purposeless display." Are we, then, ignorant of a predator's need to declare its territory? What Schiller "seems to be arguing," Bellah writes, apologetically, first calling Schiller a great poet, if only an amateur philosopher, "is that human life is riven by a series of dichotomies that play overcomes: matter and form, sense and intellect, actuality and necessity, and so forth."[5] This romantic broadening of a point too tenuous even to be called tendentious is redolent of Stanley Cavell's fatuous thesis that *King Lear* and *Othello* dissolve the epistemic problems posed by skepticism. Evidently vexed questions of philosophy and biology can be dissolved thoroughly by a natural genius too advanced to need to state them.

---

3. Ibid., 570.

4. Guthrie, *Handbook of the Collections,* 130–32.

5. Bellah, *Religion in Human Evolution,* 568.

I.5 Ritual and Religion

I'm inclined to agree with Bellah that there's more to animal (and even plant) behavior than sheer "struggle for existence." There are intrinsic as well as instrumental goals. Autonomy emerges as evolution proceeds.[6] Play is part of that. But let us not pretend selection pressures somehow stand aside. More likely is the interplay of long- and short-term interests: Parental care and sustenance make room for growth and learning, much as the womb or eggshell affords an environment cosseted from the stresses young will face in adulthood—and just as parasites lose the complex organs of their free-living forms once ensconced in some hospitable host's gut or tissue. Yes, kittens love to play, or they wouldn't do it. But what they learn is rarely irrelevant to their survival history and prospects of their lineage.

As for equality, it seems as grave an error to project idyllic, egalitarian standards on relationships in tribal cultures as it is to expect them in animal play. Frans De Waal, whom Bellah cites extensively, has done splendid work on animal empathy, especially in primates. But he never pretends that dominance hierarchies simply disappear. Species differ in their social interactions. But play is typically a way of establishing and reaffirming an order of dominance. Anyone can observe the testing among horses, dogs, and cats. If metaphors of ritual apply, it's because the testing need not lead to open, wasteful battle. But equality is rarely in question.

I'm dubious about equality in tribal relationships, on empiric as well as conceptual grounds. The notion that tribal societies are simpler and thus fairer than our own reflects contrastive abstracting from the familiar rather than close study of tribal life. "Primitive" languages are complex, not simple. Tribal people know their natural and supernatural surroundings at a level of detail that can embarrass a casual visitor—although individuals' knowledge and interests vary, of course. This is not the place and now is not the time to attempt a review of the ways in which equality of diverse sorts is advanced or constricted in every social structure. But it does seem clear that norms friendly to individual autonomy can constrain and be constrained by familial and clan authority and loyalty. Lax family structure can be hard on women, children, and the elderly. Deference to the elderly can cramp the liberties of the young.

So, conceptually, equality seems a multi-headed hydra. Industrial societies foster equality in specific domains by compromising it elsewhere: we strive to equalize opportunity and civil rights with elaborate legal and social institutions, market mechanisms, charities. The devices we deploy enhance

6. Goodman, *Creation and Evolution*, 59–61, 165–68.

41

equality here by paring it elsewhere. It's hard to deny that the same is true in tribal societies: if decisions are to be made by consensus or tradition, someone's liberty has been curtailed, and some means exist by which that outcome is effected. That's part of what Hobbes meant in urging that much is gained by foregoing a "natural" state in favor of civil society. Spinoza and Locke are not embarrassed to name what is enhanced: not just safety and security but liberty.

Bellah is passionate about his moral message: liberty is purchased at the price of equality. The ugly corollary that might have exposed the fallacy behind this zero-sum trade remains unstated: that equality is won only by the sacrifice of liberty (rather than the two enhancing one another).

Liberty, like equality, I'd suggest, has multiple dimensions. Many recent theorists, following up on a mournful thought of Isaiah Berlin's, echoing Kant's reflections on the crooked timber of humanity, have argued that any social or political arrangement sacrifices something precious. Martha Nussbaum, drawing on insights from Greek tragedy, argues to similar effect. Adam Schaff (1913–2006), the Polish Jewish philosopher, long a Stalinist enforcer, was deemed a heretic for suggesting that alienation results not simply from capital appropriation but runs deeper in the human condition—as existentialists had argued.

These theorists have forgotten that the task of politics, as Plato knew, is to coordinate goods that are inherently incommensurate yet intimately interlocked: human dignity, for example, with need; or liberty, in its diverse varieties, with privacy; individuality with community. I see no magic recipe toward such ends. But I do not believe they're unattainable. Tragedy is not inevitable, if tragedy means ultimate irreconcilability of critical goods.

Both needs and rights, in all their dimensions, are moving targets. Our capabilities (and thus our expectations) grow and change. I doubt there's just one way of optimizing outcomes fairly. But many are unjust or marred by glaring faults structurally linked with perceived or real strengths. The work of history, politically, morally, and religiously, confronts the tasks of conciliating, rectifying, optimizing, to ameliorate the human condition. This is what Jewish texts call *tikkun olam*, repairing the world. To win ground without violence or loss of ground already won demands more than a slogan. The delicacy of a task so fraught with unseen (or slighted) consequences is one good moral reason why such work cannot be relegated to evolution. But biology has some complaints to make on that score as well.

Couching moral arguments in evolutionary terms or reading evolution in moral terms is deeply problematic, as the case of social Darwinism has long made clear. But the risks are perhaps easier to miss when norms like equality seem to be at stake. Short of selective breeding of a sort that is both repugnant and impractical with human populations, evolution takes the course it takes. August Weissmann demonstrated that biological inheritance depends on changes in the germplasm, specifically, the chromosomes, as he first proposed in 1884. None of the 901 offspring of mice whose tails he docked over five generations was born with a shortened tail. Genetic variance stems from mutations, changes to the DNA and its arrangement. Use and disuse do not cause evolutionary change. No matter how I exercise, my offspring will not have bigger pecs or flatter abs. Acquired somatic traits, lying outside the genome, are not inherited. Contra Lamarck (and Bellah), cultural evolution is a metaphor, not a fact.

Pleas for balance, even in the name of play or ritual, will take hold only insofar as those addressed can make out their wisdom or appeal. Evolution, however, a charged word, often freighted with moral demands, can stand in rhetorically for powerful hypothetical imperatives, perhaps effective with an audience unresponsive to other appeals. The implicit plea: *evolve—or face extinction!* But the evolution that science validates is a piecemeal change in the genetic makeup of a population, not a choice made or neglected. Moral traits (those for which one might sensibly be praised or blamed) are not heritable. Nor, a fortiori, are moral choices.

The fall from the Edenic state Bellah evokes with his talk of play comes with the rise of agriculture, trade, and industry, cities, armies, and property and the need for its protection. His model parallels Plato's sketch of the transformation of a subsistence society to a diversified economy and stratified society. Surplus is the serpent here, creating capital and leisure but also hierarchy and hegemony. Intensifying inequities, iniquities as Bellah reads the record, provoke inevitable reactions. As economic change breeds new technologies and new social forms accelerate the transformation, new values are born. Moral visionaries that Bellah calls renouncers find the asperities intolerable. Since the civilizational processes behind the change are global, there are comparable reactions worldwide: the great movements of the Axial Age.

That age in ancient Israel and India, classical Greece, and late–first-millennium-BCE China is represented here by its religious and philosophical monuments, texts in disparate idioms linked to figures long and variously illuminated, enshrined, and obscured by sacred and secularizing history. Christianity and Islam are set aside here, at least in the explicit discussion, not fitting the Axial time frame. Bellah's story, he writes, "stops 2,000 years ago."[7] But although the Axial moment is past, it retains what Eric Voegelin called a mortgage on the present.

The Axial Age was Karl Jaspers's concept, schematized in what Arnaldo Momigliano called "the first original book on history to appear in postwar Germany." Jaspers had observed that Confucius, Lao-Tse, the Buddha, Zoroaster, the prophets of ancient Israel, and the great philosophers, tragedians, and historians of ancient Greece all lived between 600 and 300 BCE. It was an age of literacy, Momigliano notes, centralized government, advanced metal working, urban planning, and international diplomacy. "In all these civilizations," at this era, Momigliano wrote, "there is a profound tension between political powers and intellectual movements. Everywhere one notices attempts to introduce greater purity, greater justice, greater perfection, and a more universal explanation of things. . . . We are in the age of criticism."[8]

The achievements of the Axial Age are not of a piece, nor are the civilizations placed at center stage as discrete as some Hegelian analysis might suggest. Momigliano rightly stresses the tensions. This was the age not just of Greek philosophers, tragedians, and historians but also of many a sophist who shared a tragedian's outlook, influenced historians, and challenged the philosophers. These were also the years of Alexander, who gave the coup de grace to the warring Greek *poleis*, inaugurated an age of cultural fusion and diffusion, as Moses Hadas put it, and sustained philosophers like Aristotle and his school. There is no axial harmonious chorus but complexity and conflict. In ancient Israel, a Samuel could anoint a Saul but then renounce him, hewing off the head of the widow maker Agag, whom Saul had meant to spare. A Nathan could secure the throne for Solomon, having denounced the royal treachery that brought that king to birth. But perhaps these figures don't count, since they died before the Axial curtain rose.

Israel's prophets would have little meat for their message without looking to the Mosaic law and recalling Mesopotamian and Egyptian interludes. Neither Plato nor Aristotle, nor the tragedians and historians of Greece could assay the ideals of their civilization blind to the panorama of fierce individualists painted in Homer's epic of the contest of Achaians with

7. Bellah, *Religion in Human Evolution*, 599.
8. Momigliano, *Alien Wisdom*, 8–9.

a rival, Dardanian, civilization to the east—or without the lens of Homer's sequel, following the homeward journey of an isolated man, through hazards natural and supernatural: most dire, sweet promises of mindlessness and looming threats from the anti-types of civilization itself.

Some adjustments are necessary, of course. Plato, Bellah argues, should probably be read as friendlier to democracy than his critiques of it suggest. Well, we'd all like Plato to be our friend. But the truth is more complex. The awakening that led Plato to reject grounding political legitimacy on birth, or wealth, military prowess, promise or repute, eloquence, or gender, rather than wisdom and judgment, was mediated by traumatic experience with both major Athenian factions: the aristocratic pro-Spartan party might have seemed Socrates's natural allies. Plato had relatives prominent among them. But this was the party of the Thirty, discredited by that junta's excesses when it came to power after the Athenian defeat in the Peloponnesian War. Plato works hard to show that Socrates dissociated himself from them. Yet it was the restored democracy that executed Socrates. What did it say about democracy that the public assembly condemned Socrates to death by a greater plurality than found him guilty?

Democracy as Plato saw it in operation, insufficiently safeguarded by constitutional guarantees, was not unlike fascism in our historical experience. His comments, against that background, are remarkably generous: he calls liberty democracy's glory; license, its downfall. His portrait of the democratic man—consumer, self-improver, ever flitting from one desire and scheme to another, ultimately duped by demagogues, dictators, and opportunists—carries lessons no lover of liberal principles should ignore. So we adherents of democracy are not helped to an appraisal of its strengths and repair of its weaknesses by tendentious accounts that condemn Plato (as Karl Popper did, branding him an enemy of the open society and—despite Plato's brilliant analysis of the self-destructive paranoia of the tyrannical man, as the spiritual progenitor of totalitarianism). Nor are we helped by those who coat in whitewash a precious critique from an outsider.

Bellah renames Plato's Myth of the Cave "the Parable of the Cave," to highlight a perceived affinity to "similes" like the Buddhist Parable of the Blind Men and the Elephant—stifling, at a stroke, the poetic and philosophic powers that Plato uses to link argument with myth in the Myth of Gyges, the Myth of the Cave, and the Myth of Er. The shadows on the cave wall, Bellah suggests, may represent the projections of "ideologists?"—not flickering copies of unseen realities in the realm of Forms, then. There is not much room for ontology where even biology is political.

What eluded all the heroes of Bellah's reconstructed past, he laments, is the meta-truth of relativism, the equality not just of persons but of systems, at least once they pass muster and are boiled down to their essential, egalitarian message: "Great as the major figures of the axial age were, and universalistic as their ethics tended to be, we cannot forget that each of them considered his own teaching to be the only truth or the highest truth, even such a figure as the Buddha, who never denounced his rivals but only subtly satirized them. Plato, Confucius, Second Isaiah, all thought it was they and they alone who had found the final truth."[9]

So the Sophists win the day after all. The price of tolerance—and even survival—we are told, is surrender of the quest for truth and justice. One vision, if egalitarian enough, is no better than another. There is not much to learn from prophets or the Sutras, Confucius, Lao-Tse, Socrates, or Plato beyond the truths of tolerance that we already know and that the great teachers of the Axial Age only partially approached.

Austin, Norman. *Archery at the Dark of the Moon.* Los Angeles: University of California Press, 1975.

Bellah, Robert. *Religion in Human Evolution: From the Paleolithic to the Axial Age.* Cambridge, MA: Harvard University Press, 2011.

Goodman, Lenn. *Creation and Evolution.* New York: Routledge, 2010.

Guthrie, Jill. *Princeton University Art Museum: Handbook of the Collections.* Princeton, NJ: Princeton University Press, 2007.

Momigliano, Arnaldo. *Alien Wisdom: The Limits of Hellenization.* Cambridge: Cambridge University Press, 1971.

9. Bellah, *Religion in Human Evolution*, 602.

I.6 An Offensive Book

Philip Gorski

WHAT SORT OF BOOK is *Religion in Human Evolution*? What are its distinctive characteristics? And what are its wider implications, beyond the social sciences? My ultimate answer will be that it is a comparative-historical study in the sociology of religion distinguished by its attention to biological and cultural evolution, and which thereby opens a new front in the science-religion dialogue. For all these reasons, it is bound to offend. And for all these reasons, it is also bound to be misunderstood.

To begin with a misunderstanding: *Religion in Human Evolution* is not a work of theology. This is not to deny that it partakes of a certain theology. In Germany, after all, the seedbed of the social sciences was the liberal Protestant milieu. In the English-speaking world of the late nineteenth century, the social sciences were initially intertwined with the Social Gospel. In the United States, the sociology of religion began as Christian sociology, that is, as a practical branch of pastoral care. The courses in social ethics that are still taught in some Protestant seminaries are a remnant of this era of cooperation.

Sociology and the other social sciences have shed their confessional skins, asserting their scientific legitimacy within a secularized academy. Still, there is a liberal Protestant unconscious in the contemporary social sciences. And traces of this past can of course still be found in *Religion in Human Evolution*—in its attention to the interplay between religious and social ethics, its critical historical treatments of religious texts, and its effort to achieve some sort of synthesis between religion and science. But there are other counterbalancing influences as well. In particular, the influence of Durkheim, reinforced by attention to biology, leads Bellah to place considerable emphasis on ritual and myth. If *Religion in Human Evolution* is in some sense a work of liberal Protestant theology, it is a heavily reconstructed one.

However, while the theological unconscious of *Religion in Human Evolution* can and should be interrogated, it should be read, at least initially, as a work of social science. Within sociology, *Religion in Human Evolution* straddles two subfields: comparative-historical sociology and the sociology of religion. By way of contextualization, it may be helpful to say a few words about both.

The roots of comparative-historical sociology extend through the founding fathers of the discipline and, arguably, as far back as Western Antiquity. For example, its title notwithstanding, Tocqueville's *Democracy in America* is also a book about France. Nation-states needn't be the focus though. In *The Protestant Ethic and the Spirit of Capitalism* the units of analysis are religious communities—Catholicism, Lutheranism and Calvinism, in the first instance, and the historical offspring of Calvinism (e.g., Presbyterianism, Methodism, etc.) in the second. In retrospect, the civic republican tradition in Western political thought can be viewed as a sort of comparative-historical sociology *avant la lettre*. Aristotle, Machiavelli, Sydney, and Adams—all sought out the historical roots of republican regimes with an eye to the stabilization of self-government. Like Tocqueville—and unlike Weber—they wrote with a practical intent.

Courses on the sociology of religion often begin with readings from Weber and Durkheim. And rightly so. Unlike, say, Comte or Freud, they sought to explain religion sociologically, not explain it away rationalistically. Weber's approach to the subject is thoroughly comparative and historical. Struck by the brute fact of human cultural diversity, Weber invariably asked why religious life in a particular time and place was "*so und nicht anders.*" For him, religion was a historical product, not a human universal. It emerged at a particular time, what we now call the Axial Age, and out of an earlier, magical age.

Durkheim's approach was evolutionary. Unlike other early sociologists, like Spencer, Durkheim did not advance a stadial model of social development. But he did presume that human societies became more complex and differentiated over time. By this logic, the simplest—also purest—form of religion would be found in the least differentiated society. This premise authorized his treatment of aboriginal societies as living fossils that afforded vital clues about the sociogenesis of religious life as such. Religion's seedbed was ritual life, specifically, the ecstatic experience of collective effervescence that gave rise to shared beliefs about the sacred.

To these two classical approaches in the sociology of religion—the historicist and the evolutionary—we must also add a third: the phenomenological. Though its roots lay in nineteenth-century German idealism, it was first introduced into sociology over a century later by Peter Berger and Thomas Luckmann. Where Weber's approach highlighted doctrine and domination, Durkheim's ritual and *communitas*, Berger and Luckmann's emphasized experience and meaning. The wellspring of religion, they argue, is the experience of transcendence. Such experiences are numinous, ineffable. Transcendences come in various sizes. The largest ones are cosmic narratives, including religious and now also scientific ones.

Let us now situate *Religion in Human Evolution* within these subfields. Bellah's book abounds with comparisons. Multiple instances of tribal, archaic, and axial religion are compared to one another; the three types are also contrasted to one other in developmental terms. The within-type comparisons mainly emphasize similarity, so as to validate the intelligibility of each type. The cross-type comparisons mostly highlight difference, so as to illustrate the differences across types. Bellah is not inattentive to variation or continuity. However, he mostly uses comparison to establish the validity and plausibility of *Religion in Human Evolution*'s three-stage evolutionary model, not the usual strategy in comparative-historical sociology. Comparativists are typically interested in synchronic variations, not diachronic ones. Their accounts are governed by historicist tropes of contingency and conjuncture, not evolutionary ones of ontogeny and phylogeny. They are keen to dissolve unity into difference and culture into power. They rarely write with an explicitly practical extent. In all these regards, Bellah's book is an outlier.

Methodologically, however, *Religion in Human Evolution* is fairly conventional. It cites primary texts but relies heavily on secondary works. This is standard practice in comparative-historical sociology (and also in comparative history) and unavoidable when working on any long time-scale— and no extant work of comparative-historical sociology has ever attempted to work on anything like the scale of *Religion in Human Evolution. Religion in Human Evolution* often takes sides in debates between specialists, so that interested readers can revisit the specialist debate and form their own judgments. The relevant standard for such judgments is warranted belief. Some of these beliefs are narrative in form. In these cases, we prefer the best available account, knowing that it is subject to further revision. None of this is particularly controversial. Methodologically speaking, then, *Religion in Human Evolution* is normal science.

Religion in Human Evolution is written with practical as well as scholarly intent. It presents the Axial Age as a mirror for our own. Then, as now, the human species confronted a massive crisis. The crisis of our age, however, is natural as well as moral, and environmental as well as cultural. What is at stake, Bellah argues, is not just human equality, but perhaps the very survival of the human species as such. What is needed, presumably, is something like a second axial breakthrough, a renewed religious universalism that would encompass humanity's relationship to nature and to other species as well as to other persons. The evolutionary narrative, he suggests, might serve as the basic framework for intra- and cross-cultural dialogue. Here, again, Bellah breaks with mainstream social science, which (still) embraces simplistic versions of the fact/value distinction. I say simplistic, because the distinction is leaky—and in both directions. Social scientists are well aware that values can color perceptions. This is the problem of bias. What has escaped most of them is that values are also colored by facts, as we understand them. This is why rational people sometimes revise their values in light of experience.

Religion in Human Evolution may also be seen as a modern synthesis of the three main approaches to the sociological study of religion, one that builds on recent advances in our understanding of human evolution, cognition, and history. As such, it not only surpasses the sociological classics themselves, but previous syntheses as well. For instance, where Durkheim's theory of religion appealed to a quasi-Spencerian understanding of evolution, Bellah's is premised on a fully Darwinian one (albeit of a somewhat heterodox variety). Likewise, where Weber's studies of the world religions were based mainly on critical textual scholarship, Bellah's draws on recent archaeological discoveries as well. Finally, where Berger and Luckmann's phenomenology is ultimately rooted in Cartesian methods of self-observation, Bellah's levels of religious consciousness draw on recent advances in neuroscience and evolutionary psychology. The influential syntheses of Geertz and Berger were partial and even superficial by comparison. From a sociological point of view, Bellah's theory of religious evolution is easily the best account now available.

Bellah's synthesis is profoundly radical. Not in the modern "*épatez le bourgeois!*" style that tickles academic egos, but in the original "getting to the root of things" sense of offending everyone with a dog in the fight. It will offend postmodernist humanists and their romanticist followers who cling to tropes of historical and cultural difference and particularity as vindications for their own projects of self-creation and their (finally) nihilistic ethics of authenticity. It will offend Darwinian fundamentalists and their new atheist acolytes, who imagine that religion is incompatible with science and indeed with civilization itself. And it will of course offend—and frighten—religious dogmatists and creationist laypeople with its insistence that religious metanarratives be placed in serious dialogue not only with scientific narratives but with other religious narratives as well. Dialogue does not preclude commitment, of course. On the contrary, it presumes such commitment. However, it also presumes openness, the possibility that one's commitments will change as a result of the dialogue itself. Dialogue of this sort is of course very difficult, intellectually and emotionally, because belief is entangled with identity and community, and the unsettling of belief threatens our conception of self and ties to others.

Bellah's book does not leave academic intellectuals unscathed atop Olympus. On the contrary, anthropologists will undoubtedly take umbrage at Bellah's unabashed developmentalism—at his claim that social evolution involves moral evolution, however crooked the spiral. Religious studies scholars, whose favorite pastime these days seems to be deconstructing their own object of study, will feel deeply uneasy about Bellah's claim that there is such a thing as religion as opposed to just religions or even cultural practices. And sociologists of religion, wary of interlopers, will be doubly uncomfortable about his appeal to evolutionary biology and psychology.

If Bellah transgresses the disciplinary norms and boundaries of the social sciences, however, he does so at least partly with the aim of opening up a new front in the ongoing religion-science dialogue. Until recently, this dialogue has mostly involved physicists and theologians. As for the sciences of man—biological, behavioral, and social—their relationship with theology has generally been somewhat schizophrenic. One mode has been a dialogue of the deaf between atheists and fundamentalists, who see the relationship between science and religion as an inherently conflictual and zero-sum battle between "reason" and "revelation." The other has been a dialogue of the mute, which preaches peaceful coexistence on the grounds that science and religion are non-overlapping magisteria that have nothing to say to one another.

The first half of *Religion in Human Evolution* highlights a series of developments within the natural and social sciences that open up new possibilities for a real dialogue. In this context, I can only gesture towards two of them. One is the growing recognition of emergent entities and powers within the physical, natural, and social worlds, and the grave challenges it raises for atomistic, reductionistic, and deterministic understandings of the world. Another is a revised picture of human evolution that gives a much greater role to sociality in human development and success, and to processes of group selection within the evolutionary process.

By now, it should be clear where, how, and why my reading of Bellah differs from Griffiths's. Bellah's metanarrative is the best currently available social scientific account of human religiosity. Bellah is not a functionalist. (No serious sociologist is anymore.) Rather, he is a symbolic realist. And the compatibility of Bellah's account with the Christian metanarrative speaks for it, not against it.

Where the problem of religious pluralism is concerned, *Religion in Human Evolution* is in no way incompatible with Griffiths's own stance of open inclusivism. Explicating an alien religious tradition in its own terms and feeling its intellectual, moral, and spiritual force is not tantamount to affirming or embracing it. Epistemic humility and religious commitment are not necessarily at odds with one another. On the contrary, some measure of doubt is constitutive of any deep sort of faith. Moreover, as Griffiths himself has argued, serious engagement with an alien faith may potentially reveal truths about one's native tradition.

Griffiths's claim that the emergence of a world civil society would spell the end of the church and indeed of all organized religion is a sociological non sequitur. The very notion of civil society entails a realm of autonomous association beyond state control.

Finally, there is considerable evidence that the human species has made some degree of moral progress across history, though not as much as it imagines, and not without tragic regress. Perhaps the most obvious example in our recent past is the abolition—or rather near abolition—of human slavery. Steven Pinker has recently argued that there has been a significant decline in homicidal violence over the last century, the World Wars notwithstanding. Surely, this must be accounted as progress. The survival of the human species and other life on earth cannot be a matter of moral indifference to the Christian believer. However damaged the cosmos may be, stewardship of the earth is part of a Christian's vocation.

I.7 Natural Theology, Revealed Theology, Liberal Theology

Edward Feser

CATHOLICS PROBABLY QUOTE CHESTERTON too frequently. But then, he is nothing if not quotable: even when he was wrong he could find the perfect aphorism to sum up an idea. He was better still when he was right, as when he wrote that "paganism was the largest thing in the world and Christianity was larger; and everything else has been comparatively small."[1] Given the theme of this symposium, we might, for "paganism," read *natural theology*, as developed in Neoplatonic and Aristotelian thought. For "Christianity," we might read Christian *revealed theology*, articulated in language derived from those Greek philosophical traditions—grace perfecting nature in the intellectual realm. And for "everything else" since then, we might read *liberal theology*.

Thomas Joseph White suggests that Robert Bellah's *Religion in Human Evolution* is "arguably the greatest ever work of liberal Protestant theology." That is no small thing, my suggested paraphrase of Chesterton notwithstanding. But the significance, and limitations, of such an achievement can properly be understood only by contrast with the other two members of our triad. Fr. White criticizes liberal Protestantism for being open to all truth "except that of divine revelation." Yet liberal theology is not even as open as that. It has closed itself not only to revealed theology, but also to natural theology; and it has closed itself off to the former *precisely because* it has closed itself off to the latter.

Such a charge might seem surprising. Natural theology, after all, is the project of showing that certain fundamental truths of religion—the

---

1. Chesterton, "The Catholic Church and Conversion," 109.

existence and nature of God, for example—can be established via rational arguments independently of any purported source of divine revelation. And isn't the whole point of liberal theology to rationalize Christianity by stripping it of its allegedly revealed content? Isn't it precisely in the business of replacing revealed theology with a purely natural theology?

It is not; or at least, it is not in the business of any sort of natural theology that would have been recognizable to such classical practitioners of the discipline as Aristotle, Plotinus, Avicenna, Maimonides, or Aquinas. These thinkers were committed to metaphysical theses that make it intelligible how the natural world points necessarily to a divine cause. For the Neoplatonist, it is because that world contains multiple things, and things which are composite, and whatever is multiple or composite must find its source in that which is absolutely One (in the sense that would come to be enshrined in the doctrine of divine simplicity). For the Aristotelian, because the world is changing, change involves the actualization of potential, and only what is a "purely actual" Unchanging Changer can ultimately account for how any potential is actualized. For the Thomist, it is because every created thing is made up of an essence distinct from its "act of existence," and can be maintained in being only by an Uncaused Cause whose essence just *is* pure being or existence.

All of this metaphysical apparatus was swept aside by Descartes and the other founders of modern philosophy—not (some of us would argue) on the basis of a successful philosophical refutation of the views in question, but more in the interests of an essentially political reorientation of Western thought away from the speculative and toward the practical. In particular, where the study of nature is concerned, the moderns focused only on what might facilitate the prediction and control of natural processes—those aspects of nature which might be captured using the mathematical modeling techniques of Galileo and Newton. This methodological stipulation gradually morphed into a purported metaphysical discovery. The methods of natural science, as the moderns conceived of it, would ever afterward be regarded as giving us not only an especially *useful* description of nature, but an *exhaustive* description—a description of *all there is* to nature, or at least of all that could actually be *known* about nature.

Now, this description includes none of the metaphysical categories—actuality and potentiality, formal and final causes, essence and existence, and the like—by which classical natural theology reasoned from the natural world to God. It is no surprise, then, that it became the conventional wisdom in modern Western thought, cemented into its foundations by Hume and Kant, that we *could not* reason from the world to God, that the natural order is metaphysically self-contained and in need of no divine cause.

Liberal theology begins by accepting this conventional wisdom. That is one reason it does not amount to a return to natural theology, stripping from our philosophical knowledge of God the claims of revelation Christianity had brought. The conception of nature to which the liberal theologian is committed is more or less the same as that of the atheist, insofar as it makes a metaphysical inference from the world to God impossible.

But the "theology" in natural theology is no less radically transformed by the liberal theologian than the "natural." From Schleiermacher onwards, liberal theology would typically seek its foundations not in the objective natural order but in the subjective, human psychological order—in man's "feeling of absolute dependence," or the study of culture or the history of religions. That is why liberal theology is open—as classical natural theology is not—to Feuerbach's atheistic critique that theology is just disguised anthropology, and Barth's theological critique that when the liberal theologian talks about God he is really just "speaking of man in a loud voice."

Now Bellah's *Religion in Human Evolution* is, as the title alone indicates, precisely in this mold. It draws on the history of religion, evolutionary biology and psychology, sociology, anthropology, neuroscience and cognitive science—on the sciences of man, as "science" is understood by the post-Galilean, post-Newtonian metaphysical naturalist. Insofar as it represents the state of the art in these fields, summarized at magisterial length, Bellah's book may well be (as Fr. White suggests) the greatest achievement yet in liberal theology. But it will still be *liberal* theology, and thus not really *theology* at all. It does not take us beyond the natural world to God; indeed, it does not take us even beyond man.

It was only natural that the rise of liberal theology gave way historically to what has become the received view among the Western intelligentsia—that religion is an entirely man-made phenomenon with nothing to teach us about objective reality. (If communists are liberals in a hurry, perhaps the liberal theologian is a patient atheist!) The work of a scholar like Bellah might convince such sophisticates that religion is a more *interesting* falsehood than many of them had given it credit for, perhaps even a falsehood that serves fundamental human needs and is therefore unlikely entirely to disappear. What it cannot do is rescue religion from the charge that it is, for all that, a falsehood.

Natural theology, by contrast, not only purports to give us genuine knowledge of the existence and nature of God via purely philosophical arguments, but opens the door to something more—to the possibility that the God of the philosophers has revealed himself within history. That is why Aquinas characterized the claims of natural theology as the *praeambula fidei* or "preambles of faith." If reason tells us that the world has a cause outside it—a cause which, precisely because it sustains the natural order in being at every instant, might suspend that order in a miraculous way—then it also tells us that a special revelation from that cause is something it is reasonable to look for. It tells us that faith in the proper sense—trust in what we have received from God himself via knowably miraculous means—is something that can be rational.

It is precisely its dogmatic refusal to challenge the Humean and Kantian critiques of natural theology and of the possibility of miracles that keeps liberal theology from taking the claims of revealed theology seriously. Hence Fr. White is, I think, too generous when he attributes to liberal theology a "catholic aspiration to universal knowledge," at least of a non-revealed sort. On the contrary, the very greatest achievements of modern liberal theology cannot take us even as far as what the Greeks had already discovered 2,300 years ago.

Chesterton, G.K. "The Catholic Church and Conversion." In *The Collected Works of G.K. Chesterton.* San Francisco: Ignatius, 2011.

PART II

What is a Person?

Christian Smith

II.1 The Person Before God

Phillip Cary

THE CONCEPT OF A person came into Western thought from Christian theology. This does not mean no one used the Latin word *persona*, or its derivatives in other languages, prior to the existence of Christianity. It does mean that it was in Christian theology that this word first came to play an important role in the work of thought, as a topic of intense reflection and controversy. The use of "person" as a central term in human self-under-standing derives from this history of theological reflection and controversy. It came to us from the doctrine of the Trinity, and its usage to this day is marked by its original purpose of referring to God as three persons, Father, Son, and Holy Spirit. It is a reminder that when we talk about ourselves, we are trying to understand that which is most irreducibly important and lovely in the world, an image of divine mystery and beauty.

There are many points of interest, not to say ironies, about the rela-tionship between Trinitarian theology and our self-understanding as per-sons. The first to bear in mind is the application of a general point made by Thomas Aquinas: it may be admitted in some way that the things God created are like God, but it may not be admitted in any way that God is like the things of creation.[1] When we speak of likeness between us and God, therefore, our discourse should be asymmetrical, comparing ourselves to God in some way but not vice versa. Even when we say God has being, Thomas teaches, we are speaking only analogously, using the familiar term "being"—which we know how to use of created beings such as ourselves—in a way that is quite inadequate to express the reality of God. Unlike us, he is not one being among others. So also with the term *person*. We are persons like God, but God is not a person like us. The word *persona*, which

1. Aquinas, *Summa Theologica*, I, 4.3 ad 4.

had a familiar meaning in ordinary Latin, is quite inadequate to express the reality of Father, Son, and Holy Spirit. But as Augustine said, we need to use *some* such term or other if we are to engage in Trinitarian theology at all, rather than being forced into silence.

So we speak of three persons. For Christians do not speak of three Gods. We use the term *person* precisely because there is no *kind* of thing that there are three of in God, as Augustine explains. No species term (such as *god* or *deity*) can be used in the plural when describing the one true God. Nor, as the Athanasian Creed puts it, can we use abstract substantive terms in the plural.

So that tells us something about why the three persons in God are not like any persons in the created world. The word *person* does not refer to a kind of thing that there are three of in God. Even the phrase *three persons* is misleading unless it is more or less immediately dissolved into some such phrase as "Father, Son, and Holy Spirit." It is a label whose ordinary grammar must not be extrapolated in our confession of the Trinity, as if Father, Son, and Holy Spirit were three individuals of a species called "person."

Still less does the theological usage of the term invite us to ask what the three persons are made of. This is not only because of the familiar point that God is immaterial, not made up of some material or other. More fundamentally, God is simple, not constituted or composed out of any parts whatsoever, not even immaterial parts. This is why, for example, the Christian theological tradition has never spoken of God as having a soul, which is part of the composition of embodied living creatures. Souls belong to these creatures precisely because they are by nature composite—composed of soul and body together. But the three persons of the holy Trinity are not composed of anything, not put together out of parts of any kind. Father, Son, and Holy Spirit are not parts of God (for each *is* God) nor are they themselves made up of something more basic than themselves. So it is vain for us to ask about their internal constitution. If we want to speak rightly of these three persons—to identify what constitutes them and distinguishes them—we must speak about the relations *between* Father, Son, and Holy Spirit, not what is *in* them. We must identify the Son as eternally begotten from the Father, for example, and the Father as the source of the being of the Son and Spirit.

This is a peculiar way to talk, to be sure, but we can begin to see why it has had a salutary effect on the way persons are spoken of in Western thought. To start with, it is of great importance that *person* is not a term designating a species. Although human persons can be spoken of straight-forwardly in the plural (so that "three human persons" make three humans, in contrast to the three divine persons of the Trinity, who do not add up to three divinities), still what makes human beings persons cannot be reduced to their membership in the species *homo sapiens*. No biological description of the human species can exhaust what is meant when we say that a human being is a person. A similar point holds for ancient philosophy as well as modern science: no philosophical account of human nature is sufficient to tell us what a person is, for no created nature exhausts the concept of "person." The angels and the demons are persons, but they do not share in human nature. And it is possible that one day we will find there are creatures on faraway planets who are not human but who are unmistakably persons. We already find it easy to imagine that possibility in our science fiction.

Moreover, we can already ask intelligibly, and sometimes even help-fully, what would have to be true of animals or machines for them to be persons. We can ask: what makes a dolphin or a chimpanzee more like a person than a bird or a mouse? What makes an artificial intelligence (AI) like and unlike a person? As we ask these questions, we come closer to an understanding of what kind of thing we mean by "person." But precisely the fact that the term does not originate as the designation of a nature or species helps us ask these questions more intelligently, with deeper awareness of how many questions remain open. When asking "What is a person?" our inquiry is not foreclosed by premature identification of the kind of thing we are asking about, as if it were some particular species or nature. This has a very salutary effect indeed: we who are persons do not quite know what we are, yet we know it is something important and worthy of careful inquiry. If we are Christians, we know this is because we are made in the image of God, who precisely as person is incomprehensible, not belonging to any genus or species of thing, and thus utterly unlike us. Aquinas's rule again applies: created persons are like God, but God is not like created persons.

Christian Smith's inquiry in *What is a Person?* is very much a case in point. On the one hand, though he plainly has human persons in view, his list of the causal capacities from which human personhood emerges[2] would apply to any embodied person we might meet in creation, including extra-terrestrial beings or intelligent machines. If we ever encountered a machine that displayed all thirty of the capacities on his list, for example, we would surely have to recognize it as a person. If you think this is impossible, it

2. Smith, *What is a Person?*, 42–59.

must be in part because you think many of those capacities are beyond the capability of any machine. On the other hand, Smith's holistic emergentism, in which the whole is a reality that can't be reduced to the sum of its parts or the collection of its capacities, means that human beings need not have every one of these capacities in order to be persons—a very important consideration when he comes to the topic of the dignity of persons, which he rightly avoids basing on the possession of any particular set of capacities.[3] Thus the concept of personhood is neither identified with the human species nor reduced to a particular set of capacities.

Still less is it defined by a particular internal constitution. Rather, a variety of material and bodily components (which might be quite different in an extraterrestrial person) could be the basis from which emerges the constellation of capacities that together characterize persons. In Smith's account, persons emerge from this constellation of capacities, no one of which is logically necessary for personhood, and these capacities in turn can emerge from a variety of material substrata. So what persons are is strictly defined neither by their material composition, nor by their causal capacities, nor by the species or nature to which they belong, even though all these figure importantly in what they are.

That seems to me exactly right, from a theological standpoint. What persons are are creatures made in God's image. Their material composition (or for that matter their immaterial being, in the case of the angels), their internal constitution, and the exact constellation of causal capacities they possess may differ from one kind of person to another, from one species of creature to another. But what they have in common is the divine image.

And what does that mean? It means persons are related in a distinctive way to God, a way different from all other creatures. Just as the three divine persons are constituted by their relation to one another (begetting, begotten, proceeding, etc.), so created persons are defined above all by their relations with God and with one another, not by their internal constitution or the components and capacities from which they emerge. In biblical terms, persons are those who can become the neighbors of other persons: those to whom other persons owe love, those whose goods other persons may not covet, against whom a person must not bear false witness, and so on. Persons are those creatures who belong in these ethically structured social relationships. And they belong in ethically structured relationships

3. Ibid., 446–53.

with God: bound by his law, partners in the covenant he has established, analogous (as Scripture insists) to his children or his bride.

All this is immensely useful to sociology at a time when the concept of "soul" has fallen out of scientific usage. Here the theological tradition has turned out to have conceptual resources the philosophical tradition lacks. It is worth bearing in mind that "soul," ever since Aristotle, was a biological rather than religious category. For well over a millennium it was taken for granted that animals had souls, just like the Bible said, because everything that had life had a soul in Aristotelian biology. The difference between a carcass and a living animal is precisely that the latter still has its soul. It was only after Descartes that people began to think animals might not have souls, and it was only with the demise of Aristotelian science in modernity that "soul" gradually ceased to be a biological concept and started to sound like a specifically religious concept. When that happened, the notion that humans are special because they have a unique kind of soul—a rational, immortal soul rather than a vegetative or animal soul—also became less and less useful in sciences like psychology and sociology, as well as in most varieties of philosophy.

And that's when the term *person* came into its own. Smith traces his own personalism to movements whose roots go back little more than a century,[4] to a time when the concept of soul was clearly no longer useful in empirical science. So if the empirical sciences are to give us any kind of insight into who we are, they will surely need some concept other than "soul." The concept they need, Smith argues, is "person." Perhaps, indeed, as he and other personalists imply, it is a concept they inevitably do use, without quite acknowledging it or doing justice to it.

And justice must be done. "Person," unlike "soul," is an inescapably ethical category. To recognize someone as a person is immediately to recognize obligations, claims, and responsibilities toward this other, this neighbor. Hence the concept of person is entangled with a rich set of ethical implications that (Smith rightly argues) empirical sciences like sociology ignore at their peril. You have to do justice to persons, even when you're simply studying them. The insistence on treating "person" as an ethically-loaded concept was inscribed indelibly into Western thought, about a century before the rise of the movements explicitly calling themselves "personalism," by Immanuel Kant, who gave us powerful formulations of the dignity of

4. Ibid., 98–102.

persons as rational beings, subjects of the moral law, who must never be treated simply as means but always respected as ends in themselves.

It was through Kant that the concept of "person" made its emphatic entry into ethics from theology. Having removed the concept of the soul from the realm of empirical phenomena, he needed some term to designate the perceptible presence of rational beings who are subjects of law, justice and respect, and the word he came up with was *person*. In fact for Kant *person* and *rational being* were interchangeable terms, precisely because his ethics was not concerned with human nature and its specific characteristics but with what follows from the notion that a particular being (of whatever species) was possessed of rationality. Which goes to show that his concept of person was in fact taken over ultimately from Christian theology, where for a millennium and a half the standard definition of "person" had been "individual substance of rational nature."

The definition comes from Boethius in the sixth century, and it is already a product of theology at its most philosophical. Boethius was the most learned Latin writer of his time, the only one who displayed an extensive knowledge of logic, composing commentaries on the logical writings of Aristotle and Porphyry, for example. His five theological tractates are devoted in large part to the work of regularizing the logic of Trinitarian and christological discourse—sorting out the logical relations between terms like *nature, substance,* and *person.* The upshot (which I must drastically condense here) is roughly this: "substance," like "nature," is what there is only one of in the Trinity. This is because there is only one divine nature and also because, most importantly, Father, Son, and Holy Spirit share one being or essence (*ousia* in Greek, *essentia* or *substantia* in Latin). This is a key contention of orthodox theology deriving from the Nicene Creed's confession that the Son is "of one being" (*homo-ousios*) with the Father, a crucial term translated into Latin as "consubstantial" (*consubstantialis*). So "substance" derives from the Latin term, *substantia,* which renders the Greek word for being, *ousia.*

This generates one of the linguistic confusions Boethius must sort out. The etymological equivalent of *substantia* in Greek is *hypostasis*: Both words are formed from roots meaning "to stand under," as when we speak of the underlying being of something. But *hypostasis* in Greek theology, it turns out, was used for what is three in God, while *substantia* in Latin was used for what was one in God. In other words, *hypostasis* was equivalent to what Boethius meant by the phrase, "*individual* substance." Talk of "three hypostases" had caused no end of confusion and trouble since the fourth century, both in Greek and in Latin translation, so Boethius was fortunate to have another term, native to the Latin tradition, to designate what was three in God: *persona*. (There's a Greek equivalent, *prosopon*, but it is not so prominent as *hypostasis* in Greek theology or *persona* in Latin theology.) Boethius defined *persona* in a way to make the connection with Greek trinitarian terminology: A person is an "individual substance," which is to say a *hypostasis*. But the term does not apply to just any *hypostasis*. A dog or horse is a *hypostasis*, an individual substance; so is a tree or a table. *Persona* is more restricted than that: It means an individual substance *of rational nature*—i.e., exactly what Kant meant, centuries later, by a rational being.

Now all this logical sorting out is a bit too neat, for reasons we've already noticed. The three persons of the Trinity are not individual substances of any kind of nature, as Augustine saw. If that were literally true then they'd be three distinct individuals, making three distinct gods. But as Augustine remarked, we need to say something, and *persona* is a term Latin theologians had been using for two centuries already by the time Augustine wrote, a century before Boethius. And it was handy, for reasons that go beyond Boethius's logical sorting out of terms to the original meaning of *persona* in ordinary Latin.

Persona, from *per-sonare*, to sound or speak through, originally meant "mask." As a result it came to refer to the characters in a drama, because in ancient theater the characters on stage wore masks. The Latin for "masks of the drama," *dramatis personae*, is still used today at the beginning of many playbills to introduce the list of characters. It is in this dramatic sense that the word *persona* seems to have appealed to Tertullian, who first used it to describe what is three in the Trinity. Loosely connected to this dramatic sense is a grammatical sense, still evident when we talk about first person, second person, and third person pronouns or verb forms. In a drama, one character speaks to another as I (first person) speak to you (second person), observed by him or her (third person). What all three persons have in common, Tertullian noted, is that in Latin they are spoken of in masculine or feminine gender but not neuter: as *unus*, not *unum*; roughly translated: as some*one*, not some*thing*. That's the distinction, I take it, that Boethius is trying to capture when he adds "of rational nature" to the notion of "individual substance." But perhaps we will do better to dwell for a moment on this earlier, less tidy and philosophical way of thinking about it: a person is someone, not something, the sort of one (or *unus*) who speaks to another one (a second person) as characters who belong together in the same drama.

In the Bible, God is portrayed as such a one: one who speaks and is spoken to, one who enters into ethical relations of covenant and promise and commandment, one whose word is to be believed and obeyed, but also one to whom may be addressed words of appeal, complaint, thanks, and praise. When Christ comes into the world, he also is one who speaks in prayer and praise to God his Father, and who in turn is spoken to. And he promises his disciples that his Father will send someone else—another *unus*—the Holy Spirit, to teach them all things and guide them into all truth. So God plays the role of three characters in the biblical drama, which is to say, each one of these three persons is God. That seems to be the underlying sense of the Latin theological term *persona*.

So we see why it's not simply misleading to define persons as individual substances of rational nature, even though such a definition can only be applied analogically, not literally, to the persons of the Trinity, for whom it was originally intended. For classical philosophy *rational* was not a reductive term but an expansive one, full of implications: a rational substance is one capable of speaking and understanding, learning and erring, willing and refusing—precisely the kind of *someone* who can take part in a drama. And we can see why, so defined, the term *person* does not have to be tied to a particular species of being: the rational *someones* in classical drama could be gods, nymphs, or satyrs as well as human beings, just as the characters in our science fiction stories can include extraterrestrial beings who are clearly persons, even if they are hardly human (think of the weirdly shaped denizens of the Mos Eisley cantina in the first *Star Wars* film).

Yet we can also see why a person is typified by certain characteristic capacities, those which make participation in drama possible: rationality, for example, implies the capacity to use language and speak for oneself, to understand oneself and others, to desire knowledge of the truth. These are the kind of capacities that figure prominently in Smith's list of thirty—but their derivation from the dramatic life of persons shows why it would not be wise to insist on precisely this particular list, as if one capacity more or less than thirty would be a problem. It's not the exact list of capacities that matters, but the ability to participate in the drama. And finally, we can see why persons as *individual* substances are characterized not by their internal constituents—not even by their rational nature, which they have in common with other persons—but by their interaction with other persons in the drama. Here we see the ethical character of individual persons in action, in their speaking and hearing, understanding and misunderstanding each other, hating and loving one another.

And this is how God is characterized in Holy Scripture. Though not literally a person in Boethius's sense, the God of Israel has literally taken part in the drama of human life in the triune fashion that the biblical drama attests. And that, most fundamentally, is why we should think of ourselves also as persons. The history of the term that I have sketched does have its ironies, as I suggested at the beginning. It starts out as a rather ordinary term for grammatical and dramatic speakers, then is applied to the incomprehensible triune reality of the God who descends among us to take part in our dramas and even our grammatical speech, and then finally it is re-applied to us, as those who are made in the image of this God. By the time it comes back to us, it has gained a richness, depth, and dignity that goes beyond all human drama, for it situates the drama of human life within a theo-drama rooted in the eternal life of God, Father, Son, and Holy Spirit.

No wonder sociologists have a bit of a problem with it. As every form of personalism recognizes, the notion of *person* brings with it the notion of *dignity*. And as the theological history of the term suggests, that dignity is hard to separate from our dramatic relationship with the incomprehensible God who made us in his own image. This is heavy baggage for the notion of "person" to carry, as it originates in a realm beyond empirical investigation and puts serious ethical constraints on any scientific work. Sociologists and their investigations are inevitably part of the drama of persons speaking, listening, understanding, and interacting with other persons. They are not merely spectators, like an audience observing the drama from outside. This inevitable involvement in the ethically fraught drama of human life threatens the ideology of value-free science that many sociologists believe ought to be normative for their work.

In this regard Smith is proposing a major revision of sociology's self-understanding, driven by convictions that may not strictly require a theological conception of persons but certainly point in that direction. I would say: Christian theology helps us see why we have the intuition that persons *matter*, ultimately and irreducibly. And apart from this theological conviction it may be difficult for Smith to explain why we should insist on upholding that intuition as a criterion for measuring the adequacy of work in empirical sciences like sociology. Why not freely use sociology to measure, predict, and manipulate masses of human beings, if it serves some purpose of ours? To say why not, I think we need some notion that the drama in which persons participate is not an illusion or a fiction, not simply one of the many stories we like to tell ourselves, but is situated within the cosmic theo-drama, the real story of the world, which Scripture calls the gospel of Jesus Christ. It is a drama in which persons are ultimately and irreducibly important, lovely, and good, because it is a drama in which the three persons of the Trinity take part. Sociologists too are persons in that drama; they belong to the story of Jesus Christ whether they recognize it or not, and that is why they too have an ineluctable intuition, often unacknowledged, that they have an obligation to do justice to the persons they study.

Aquinas, Thomas. *Summa Theologica.* 5 vols. Translated by the Fathers of the English Dominican Province. Notre Dame, IN: Christian Classics, 1948.

Smith, Christian. *What is a Person?* Chicago: University of Chicago Press, 2010.

II.2 Revelation's Nature

David Yeago

PHILLIP CARY'S EXCELLENT OVERVIEW of the theological roots of personalism ends by raising a question about the plausibility of Christian Smith's proposal to the social sciences apart from "some notion that the drama in which persons participate is not an illusion or a fiction, not simply one of the many stories we like to tell ourselves, but is situated within the cosmic theo-drama, the real story of the world, which Scripture calls the gospel of Jesus Christ."

This is, of course, a classic conundrum that arises at nearly every point in the Christian engagement with post-Christian modernity. In this response, I want to comment on this conundrum from the viewpoint of a Christian theologian. It might be described as a little exercise in Augustinian social theory, for which the doctrine of original sin is a crucial interpretive tool.

The conundrum in question can be stated in this way: there are certain perceptions of the world and of human beings within the world that now seem essential to the preservation of any decent or humane culture and society. Many of these perceptions arose, as a matter of historical fact, in an explicitly Christian cultural setting and sometimes from very specific and even technical considerations of Christian theology. It's not only Christians who judge these perceptions to be morally indispensable. But how are these perceptions to be sustained and defended apart from the setting of Christian belief within which they arose?

David Bentley Hart's recent writing has cautioned us against the easy assumption that these perceptions have somehow been definitively extracted from their original Christian context and can now endure as permanent possessions of the post-Christian mind. Is it reasonable to expect, for example, that a culture that does not believe that human life is a gift of the Creator and that every human being is created in the image of God, will find sufficient reason to care, over the long haul, about the fate of the unborn, the old and unproductive, the expensively ill, and the mentally impaired?

The perennial response to this question is that Christian societies and Christian thinkers may have been in an especially favorable situation in which to achieve certain perceptions, but some of these perceptions are not inherently faith-dependent. There are insights of which human reason is in principle capable which are nonetheless difficult for finite human reason to achieve—all the more so given the confusion of fallen human life. Christian revelation gives believers a place to stand from which it is possible to see also the rationally accessible truth more clearly, and once such truth has been seen, it can be explained and defended by properly philosophical arguments.

This response, though true, promises little help in the struggle for cultural-political decency. Rational or philosophical argument is not, unfortunately, a royal road along which truth may travel serenely to take its throne. For fallen creatures, the path of reason is a hard road, clogged with obstructions, obscured by the shifting sands of fashion and the proliferating kudzu of delusion, offering endless attractive byways that lead to bad places. As St. Thomas Aquinas put it, through the fall the rational nature is wounded by ignorance, ill will, weakness, and irrational desire, which hinder it from achieving its proper good.[1] This is no less true of intellectuals and academics than it is of common folk; even where highly developed as a skill, the capacity for following rational argument to a conclusion tends to be morally fragile and selectively employed. As Gilbert Meilaender once wrote, "Admission to college or university is not a ticket out of the cave."[2]

Another consideration is relevant here. Smith argues that there is a rationally available knowledge of persons that is practically significant; that is, it has implications for the ways in which persons should be viewed and treated. In that respect, he is presenting something like a natural law argument. This is a good thing to do, but it is important to remember that our knowledge of the natural law is not primarily theoretical. As the Thomist philosopher Yves Simon put it, we know the natural law not chiefly by the way of cognition but by the way of inclination. Simon gives the example

1. Aquinas, *Summa Theologica* I–II, 85, 3.
2. Meilaender, *Theory and Practice of Virtue*, 83.

of a businessman who is approached with a deal that looks perfect on the surface. The would-be partner is plainly smart and appealing. Yet the businessman turns down the deal "[b]ecause the fellow, excuse me, stinks." Simon explains: "There is an inclination in the honest conscience of a man trained in justice which makes him sensitive to the unjust even when he is completely unable to explain his judgment."[3]

It is on the whole a good thing that we know the natural law in this way, by inclination, since the way of theory is slow, difficult, and not everyone's thing. However, it also makes knowledge of the natural law a chancy and intrinsically imperiled business. After the fall, the wounds of sin weaken the natural inclination of the human creature to the good. The inclination is not erased, because it arises from the essential principles of human nature, but obstacles are put in its way: confusion of mind, weakness of spirit, and an ever-proliferating tangle of contrary inclinations.

Moreover, since the knowledge of the natural law is not most directly available through theoretical reason, it becomes very difficult to restore it when it has been lost. When the "training" of the conscience of which Simon speaks breaks down or is never acquired, there is little hope that even the clearest reasoning will make up the loss. Here the moral formation of the individual and the cultural health of the community are inextricably intertwined. Natural law is not known as a rational system on the basis of which the historically disembodied mind can impose an abstract justice on the world. Collectively, living in communities, we know the natural law by way of the accumulation of concrete perceptions and discernments whose general pattern and significant high points are embodied and remembered in that complex form of corporate memory called tradition. When Simon speaks of a conscience "trained" in justice, it is initiation into the moral tradition of a commonwealth to which he refers.

Such traditions are of course imperfect; they arise out of the perceptions and judgments of fallen human creatures plagued by ignorance, ill will, weakness, and irrational desire. They develop over time, and may indeed move towards more adequate perceptions, but they cannot be rendered faultless or infallible. Perhaps the best that can be said of them is that they are likely to be more adequate to reality overall than the clever ideas of an unformed mind. At any rate, however, human societies in search of moral and social decency have little else to go on. When moral traditions are globally discredited or simply cease to be passed on from generation

3. Simon, *Tradition of Natural Law*, 128.

to generation, they are not replaced by a system of rational morality. They are replaced by the delusional inventions of the fallen human spirit, which seeks to impose on the world an order that corresponds to its desires.

None of these considerations is intended as a criticism of Christian Smith's book. My goal has been rather to suggest the difficulty and the distinctive drama of his enterprise. *What is a Person?* is an impressive work of social theory, but it is also inevitably a rhetorical undertaking, an attempt to persuade a specialized audience, the community of social scientists, to surrender theoretical models (and the world views associated with them) from which many practitioners of social science draw much of their sense of professional identity and dignity, and to adopt in their place a model (and an associated world view) that will at first glance seem to many tainted with unscientific moralism and metaphysics—with religion lurking in the background. All this in an academic culture that has tended for decades to view detachment from moral traditions—if not downright hostility to the Western moral tradition—as a condition of scientific objectivity.

Such an enterprise is by no means doomed to fail, but it faces enormous difficulties. From the perspective of "Augustinian social science," models and world views that obscure the reality of the person do not typically sit lightly on the surface of the mind, ready to be dislodged cleanly by a better argument. They have complex and obscure relations to the tangle of illusion and disordered desire that resides deep in the fallen human heart. A "civic" rhetorical project like that of Professor Smith has the difficult task of struggling with a deep disorder that it cannot cure, but only palliate and restrain. It would be worthwhile to reflect more explicitly on the nature of such rhetoric and the means of persuasion at its disposal.

Only divine grace can actually begin to cure the distemper of the heart, and that comes with a very different sort of rhetoric, the rhetoric of the gospel, to which Professor Cary's paper refers at its conclusion.

Aquinas, Thomas. *Summa Theologica*. 5 vols. Translated by the Fathers of the English Dominican Province. Notre Dame, IN: Christian Classics, 1948.
Meilaender, Gilbert C. *The Theory and Practice of Virtue*. Notre Dame, IN: University of Notre Dame Press, 1984.
Simon, Yves. *The Tradition of Natural Law: A Philosopher's Reflections*. New York: Fordham University Press, 1999.

II.3 On Being Human

Candace Vogler

CHRISTIAN SMITH'S *WHAT Is a Person?* is a tremendously ambitious attempt to restore something that has gone missing in contemporary Anglophone work on social life: humans. More precisely, he is interested in seeing social science take the person as the central focus of study. I am not a social scientist. My field is philosophy. And so I cannot speak to the exact character of the intervention Smith makes in his discipline. But that intervention is supported by a lot of metaphysics and epistemology, and those areas are a little closer to home for me. I mean this talk as a friendly philosopher's addendum to Smith's work.

I will begin with some remarks about emergence and head toward a discussion of generality—how to understand the size or scope or kind of claim that is being made, how to see the way in which it is general. If I understand him, getting the character of the generality in Smith's account right is key to evaluating critical realist personalism as a methodology for the social sciences. My hope will be to argue that Smith's deployment of emergence may not be philosophically necessary for the larger project, even though the scientific idiom of his work on emergence could help the account play well with social scientists.

Smith's focus is on persons. I take it that, by "the person," Smith means "the human being." He writes:

> By person I mean a conscious, reflexive, embodied, self-transcending center of subjective experience, durable identity, moral commitment, and social communication who—as the efficient cause of his or her own responsible actions and interactions—exercises complex capacities for agency and intersubjectivity in order to develop and sustain his or her own incommunicable self in loving

relationships with other personal selves and with a nonpersonal world. That, in any case, is what a normal person is, a person who has developed normally.[1]

As near as I can tell, Smith does not rule out the possibility that there might be nonhuman persons. If there is a reason to deny that nonhuman animals might count as Smithian persons, it will be because we think that other animals are not reflexive, or do not have the capacity for love or moral commitment. Now, it's certainly the case that contemporary study of the social lives of nonhuman animals draws on the resources of social science and sets out to understand the communication, inter- and intragroup activities, individual capacities, and intelligence of, say, crows by trying to determine how their higher-level cognitive activities emerge in the social world of the flock. The students of highly intelligent nonhuman animals, as near as I can tell, find specific—that is, species-determined—analogues for love and codes of conduct among the animals they study, and individual members of very smart species are certainly durable centers of subjective experience and the efficient causes of what they do (on the modern understanding of efficient causality, at least).

Many philosophers hold that nonhuman animals are conscious. Where most nontheist philosophers go these days to find what makes humans unlike crows or domestic dogs is toward self-reflexive self-consciousness in philosophy of mind, or toward moral culpability and accountability. Other animals can be fierce, dangerous, or inconvenient, the thought goes, but they cannot be wicked. That is our special gift. And it may be ours because we have the self-conscious, self-reflexive capacity to evaluate what we do in light of standards that would appear to be entirely alien to dolphins and chimpanzees.

By Smith's lights persons are real, emergent entities.

Emergence is a notoriously slippery philosophical notion. It is usually deployed in philosophy of physical science (for example, in arguing that chemical valences are emergent properties of subatomic particles). Most philosophers in these fields take it that emergence is primarily an epistemic notion rooted in the imperfections of our understanding of complex systems. Some arguments for epistemological emergentism are based on a point about prediction—emergent properties are features of complex systems which could not be predicted, in practice, at least, on the basis of understanding the features of, and the laws governing, the elements or parts

1. Smith, *What is a Person?*, 61.

of the preemergent state. Other variants of epistemological emergentism argue instead that emergent properties are systematic features of complex systems governed by their own laws—laws that do not govern the elements or processes of the preemergent state.

It is possible to hold either of these views while denying ontological emergentism—the view that emergent properties characterize metaphysically distinct kinds of entities or processes that are differently real than the stuff of the preemergent state. Smith wants the stronger ontological understanding of emergence, and treats emergent properties as belonging to distinct levels of reality.

As is generally true of those who hold some version of ontological emergentism, Smith does not only state that we can't predict the characteristics of the emergent state from the preemergent state. Nor does he stop at the idea that emergent properties are systematic features of complex systems that do not exhibit the features, or obey the laws, that govern the elements and processes belonging to the preemergent state. Smith also claims emergent properties are fundamental features of metaphysically distinct entities that influence the features characteristic of the preemergent state.

Smith wants lower-level entities with distinctive causal capacities that relationally interact with each other to give rise to some higher-level entity through the emergence process. The higher-level entity, in turn, exercises causal capacities downward, influencing the lower-level entities. Moreover, he does not want the emergent entity to destroy any of the underlying entities found in the preemergent state, or to destroy the causal powers that belong to the entities at the basal, preemergent level.

A number of fairly powerful objections have been raised against ontological interpretations of emergent properties in philosophy of science. The thrust of many of these objections goes like this: since the best grounds for insisting that emergent properties characterize ontologically distinct entities come from being able to show that the interactions of emergent features of complex systems alter the processes and elements of the preemergent state, those who argue for ontological emergence must be doing so on the basis of having established causal tendencies governing both the emergence of properties and causal tendencies linking the emergent properties with the elements of the preemergent state. (And then things become very complicated, depending upon how the opponent of ontological emergentism understands the nature of causation.)

To make a long and math-heavy story short, if we can track both the "upward" causal processes by which emergent properties emerge, and the "downward" causal processes by which emergent properties interact with the elements of the preemergent state, then it isn't clear why one would insist that emergent properties occupy a different level of reality from the preemergent properties. All of the properties of the complex system—preemergent and emergent—are drawn together in a single causal nexus. Nothing is lost in the process of emergence. Opponents of ontological emergentism want good reasons to deny that what the ontological emergentist has provided is simply a map of the structure of a single, complex causal system.

Once Smith has both upward and downward causation in place, he has located the preemergent and emergent properties, processes, and entities in a single causal nexus where the emergent features interact causally with the basal features without destroying the entities or features that characterize the base. It is one thing to argue that we can't reduce items occupying a single causal nexus one to another. That is easy to argue. It is even susceptible to mathematical proof, in some examples from chemistry and physics. It is quite another to insist that items occupying a single causal nexus belong to different levels of reality. To do so requires developing an account of different levels of reality such that they can interact causally with one another without ceasing to be different levels of reality, and paying very close attention to the kind of causality at issue.

One great thing about physical science is that any given established field of physical science is law-governed and provides fairly determinate accounts of the entities and happenings of concern in the relevant science. So if we are interested in, for example, the emergence of water and salt obtained by mixing hydrochloric acid with sodium hydroxide, chemists can tell you what happened and how. They can also tell you the ways in which salt and water are distinct from hydrochloric acid, and from sodium hydroxide, and can explain to you the many ways in which neither water, nor salt, nor water-and-salt can be properly treated as the sum of some effects of the individual elements that reacted to produce water and salt. The chemical reaction is not reducible. In spite of this, chemical reactions do not involve distinct levels of reality even when the emergent elements trigger additional reactions—that is, even if there is both "upward" and "downward" causality.Add water or salt to either sodium hydroxide or else hydrochloric acid and all you get is a watered down or saltier version of the stuff you had before.

I have no idea how to do the philosophy that would be required to support an account of persons as ontologically emergent entities. I have no idea how to handle the necessary account of emergence, and am at a complete loss as to how to understand the kind of upward and downward causation Smith is after. He is interested in thirty human capacities, the lowest levels of which are conscious awareness and subconscious being, the highest of which are interpersonal communion and love, aesthetic judgment and enjoyment, forming virtues, and moral awareness and judgment. The person emerges from these, and these interact with each other in complex ways. I agree that healthy adult human beings with their wits about them have the capacities on the list—at least potentially. I agree that how a person responds to herself and her world not only involves the exercise of such powers, but also influences the nature of the powers themselves. This is surely part of what is meant by insisting that the way to form virtues is by performing virtuous acts. But I think that trying to treat these points on the model of ontological emergentism does a disservice to the strength and power of Smith's account.

As near as I can tell, the problem stems from an unacknowledged commitment to something called "methodological individualism." There are two principal aspects of methodological individualism:

1. The attempt to understand complex entities solely on the basis of their properties.

2. The attempt to account for structured groups of entities in terms of the properties of the individual entities that make up the groups.

This seems to me to be the strategy that informs Smith's picture of ontological emergentism. He wants to understand the person in terms of the person's distinctive properties and capacities. He wants to understand structured groups of persons—families, for example—as collections of human beings who have or are charged with developing or nurturing the properties and capacities that characterize persons.

It may seem like any attempt to bring persons back to the forefront in social science will have to rely on methodological individualism. After all, what we want is for individual human beings—their special strengths and vulnerabilities—to inform the work that social scientists do on human life. But wanting to put individual human beings back into the center of social science does not entail a commitment to methodological individualism. That is, it does not require treating the special properties of persons, and how these properties relate to each other, as the philosophical bedrock of the account. Instead, one can start with an account of the human being—of humanity or human nature—and treat work on specific capacities as work on the distinctive powers and challenges faced by the human being. One can start at the top, and see the detailed work on moral psychology as governed by the larger understanding of our kind, rather than starting with properties and trying to build up to thought about a fully realized adult human being.

Basically, you don't need to be a methodological individualist to do the kind of work Smith wants to do. And I am concerned that methodological individualism threatens some of what we can learn from Smith.

I mentioned that I was inclined to read "person," in Smith's account, as "the human being." The human being is not the same as any particular individual human being. It is not even the same as most human beings, or most human beings who have developed in some particular way. "Human being" is the name of a kind of animal—the kind that, if Aristotle and Aquinas are right, is endowed with reason and made for political life. The human being can speak a natural language, has two legs, two eyes, two hands, two feet, and so on. The human being is characterized by all thirty of Smith's capacities or powers. If an individual adult human being lacks one of these powers, then she or he lacks something that she or he is supposed to have. If a mode of social life fails to support human beings in developing such powers, then that mode of social life fails to support our humanity. This is, I take it, what Smith means by claiming that persons are human beings "who have developed normally."[2]

The use of the concept of the normal is telling. It is not that Smith is importing some suspicious idea of normalcy into his account. Rather, he is concerned about what belongs to the human being as such. This kind of normal has nothing to do with statistical averages or the vicissitudes of childhood and adolescence. His account of what belongs to us as such could be true even if individual adult human beings who routinely exercised all thirty of Smith's powers were in fact very rare.

Michael Thompson has done significant work on this topic. Smith tells us many things about "normal persons." All of these things will, I think, belong to judgments of the kind that Thompson calls "natural historical

2. Smith, *What is a Person?*, 61.

judgment,"[3] expressed in sentences that Thompson calls "Aristotelian categoricals."[4] Smith tells us what is true not just about a person—Susan, say, or Frank. He is best read as telling us how things are with the person, and, I think more accurately, given that it matters a lot to Smith that he is talking about creatures like me rather than the best and brightest individual members of the pod of whales I saw last summer, with the human being. Thompson writes:

> If I say "Water is a liquid" . . . I do seem to presuppose what are sensibly called "normal conditions." And so, "In normal conditions, water is a liquid" is a more precise and strict formulation of my thought. If, now, I go on to spell these conditions out, I will mention, e.g., room temperature. What is "normal" or "standard" is here evidently judged by reference to myself. The "normal conditions" presupposed in such a statement as "Water is a liquid" are not *normal conditions for water*—continuous bits of it will indifferently occupy any of the three states of matter—and to articulate them is not to articulate any truth about water.
>
> Now suppose I say, "Bobcats breed in spring": it is again obvious that this isn't going to happen in any particular case unless certain conditions are satisfied. . . . But, now, to articulate these conditions is to advance one's teaching about bobcats. It is not a reflection on the limited significance of one's teaching. The thought that *certain hormones are released*, or that *they live at such and such altitudes and amid such and such vegetation*, is a thought of the same kind as the thought that *they breed in spring*. The field guide and the nature documentary assign an external environment to the intended life-form, after all, and in the same "voice" they elsewhere employ in describing its bearers' inner structure and operations.
>
> These conditions are thus "presupposed" by the life-form itself, and not by the poor observing subject with his low-resolution lens.[5]

On Smith's account, the person exercises moral and aesthetic judgment, develops a sense of self, seeks loving communion with others, and so on. Each of these points can be framed as a Thompsonian Aristotelian categorical: the S seeks F; the S does G; the S has H; the S enjoys J—and so on through all thirty of Smith's capacities. Smith deploys a model of

3. Thompson, *Life and Action*, 48.

4. Ibid., 66.

5. Ibid., 72–73.

PART II—WHAT IS A PERSON?

ontological emergentism to try to show the kinks between these. But what governs the entire account is, as his title suggests, a picture of personhood. On the Thompsonian interpretation, we can get a similar result much more directly. Thompson writes:

> The same point emerges differently if we notice that by repeated application of our apparently unexciting rule of inference—"S's are F," "S's are G," ergo "S's are both F and G"—we will presumably always be able to produce a true statement of our form involving a complex conjunctive predicate that is not true of *any* member of the kind denoted by its subject, living or dead. I mean: nobody's perfect. (Will anyone say, by the way, that anything is, *ceteris paribus*, what it never is?)
>
> This may seem to cut our propositions entirely free of "the facts." But consider the ensemble of true natural historical judgments with a given kind, S, as subject; call it *the natural history of S's*. I do not doubt that many of the features attributed to S itself in this imagined "history" will also have to be attributable to many of the individual S's (attributable, that is, in the more familiar "When little Arthur sheds his teeth . . ." sort of way). To deny it would in any case make for a bold expression of Platonism. But the affirmation alone tells us nothing about the relation that any particular judgment in the "history" must have to the class of individual S's and the facts about them.
>
> The unity of subject and predicate realized in an Aristotelian categorical, "The S is F," and the act of mind expressed in it, are thus not to be compared with those realized and expressed in the English forms "Some S is F," "All S's are F" and "Most S's are F." The latter, we may say, relate directly to features of the class of individuals covered by the subject term. The former rather express one's *interpretation* or *understanding* of the life-form shared by the members of that class. This understanding may of course be shallow or deep, extensive or narrow, mostly true or largely mistaken.[6]

In short, I think that the actual metaphysical foundation of Smith's project is not to be sought in the perilous landscape of ontological emergentism. It is rather to be found in reflection on our nature—on the kinds of creatures we, specifically, are.

Why *not* use "person" rather than "human being" for this topic? After all, "human being" could be misconstrued as some strange biological categorization, whereas "person" points to higher things. "Person" seems

6. Ibid., 287–88.

to me the right term to use if you are trying to get social scientists to think seriously about what they are doing. There are important philosophical reasons for treating Smith's theoretical foundation as a teaching about the nature of the human being.

There are various critical dimensions to Smith's critical realist personalism. He wants to link moral and political aspirations with social scientific knowledge. He wants a sound causal understanding of human development, human social institutions, and the like, to be useful in the service of improving our lives and our world. The causal account he offers is an account of how things are supposed to go for human beings. All of the rich complexity of linkages between our capacities is meant as a map of the sorts of powers that a healthy adult human being needs in order to lead a full and meaningful human life. If, as I urge, we read these sentences as Aristotelian categoricals, then they detail a kind of goal that can rightly be attributed to human society. Human society ought to make possible the development and exercise of such powers, ought to recognize the dignity of human beings, and ought to be organized in such a way that each of us can rightly aspire to the higher purposes at stake in the account.

I strongly suspect that most currently existing societies fall short of this goal. That could well mean that very few human beings are straightforwardly supported in living the kinds of lives Smith argues we should be able to live. If we adopt a Thompsonian interpretation of Smith's project, then the fact that a lot of us do not get to lead the life Smith outlines allows us to say that societies that fail to support the aspirations outlined in Smith's vision are to that extent and for that reason *defective*. If, instead, Smith is just telling us what most people happen to be like, or what an average person is like, or how things are with people many of us happen to admire, then we instead need to look at how things are for people generally to assess whether Smith has got it right. Instead of giving us sentences that tell us "The Human Being has such-and-such capacities," Smith will be making tacit reference to some sort of data set, and evaluation of his project will boil down to evaluation of his work with his data set. On the Thomsponian interpretation, it could turn out that fewer than 10 percent of people live the kind of life Smith describes and Smith's account might be absolutely true.

What the rarity of moral and personal achievement in human life would show isn't that Smith had made a mistake, but rather that we are failing each other and ourselves more often than not. On the Thompsonian interpretation, in short, the term *person* becomes a way of marking how things are for an adult human being when all is as it should be for an adult human being.

There is another important philosophical reason for taking Smith's topic to be the human being rather than personhood in some general sense. There are many, many human beings who have developed normally (in both Thompson's sense of "normal" and Smith's) *their whole lives* and lack the capacities on Smith's list. Take, for example, a healthy baby. Call her "Sarah." Sarah is two months old and has developed normally her whole life. Quite frankly, Shep, the faithful family dog who is watching Sarah play on the living room rug, is more likely to exhibit some of the capacities on Smith's list than Sarah is at this stage. What accounts for Sarah's moral standing and dignity isn't that she will score well in a test measuring her ability to exercise the capacities on Smith's list. It is that she is a human being.

I have tried to urge that the sound metaphysical foundation for Smith's work is not in ontological emergentism, but is rather to be found in venerable accounts of the human being, given their strongest modern philosophical treatment in work by philosophers like Thompson. I do not know whether Thompsonian reflection on these matters will convince most social scientists to rethink their methods, but I am fairly convinced that it will help philosophers give Smith his due.

Smith, Christian. *What is a Person? Rethinking Humanity, Social Life, and the Moral Good from the Person Up.* Chicago: University of Chicago Press, 2010.

Thompson, Michael. *Life and Action: Elementary Structures of Practice and Practical Thought.* Cambridge, MA: Harvard University Press, 2008.

II.4 Religion's Rightful Claim

David Novak

CANDACE VOGLER IS CORRECT to criticize Christian Smith's use of "emergence"[1] (which she calls "a notoriously slippery philosophical notion") to counter the kind of reductionism that explains more complex entities by a reference to their simpler preconditions or causes. But how deep does her critique of Smith go?

The reductionism rejected by Smith tries to explain features of human beings such as self-consciousness and moral culpability in terms of the physical factors (primarily the struggle to survive as a species) that precede their *emergence* in the world, and without which they would not emerge at all. For reductionists, these physical factors are not only necessary preconditions *for* these features of human personhood; they are sufficient causes *of* them. One sees this in attempts to reduce the activity of thinking or "mind" to the physical entity, the brain, where thought is located (at least in our human experience of our own actions).

Such explanations so over-explain the phenomenon (the *explanandum*) they explain it away, i.e., they make it *epiphenomenal*. Reducing such activities as thinking (what is mindful) and choosing (what is willful) to merely bodily functions like eating or breathing makes these activities unrecognizable to the very humans who engage in them, and who believe these activities to be essential to their human personhood taken *as such* (as Vogler emphasizes). Smith's resistance to this reductionism puts him in the company of Dilthey (who refused to reduce *Geisteswissenschaften* to *Naturwissenschaften)* and Husserl (who distinguished phenomenology, with its bracketing of the search for antecedent causes, from "scientism"). As far as this anti-reductionist project goes, Vogler expresses *ab initio* her

---

1. Smith, *What is a Person?*, 14.

83

agreement with Smith's "tremendously ambitious attempt to restore something that has gone missing in contemporary Anglophone work on social life: humans."

So, where does Vogler disagree with Smith? Well, Smith's main point against the reductionists is Aristotelian: a whole is greater than the mere sum of its parts. This is true of any living being, especially any animal (*zoòn* in Greek), and is certainly true of humans who are speaking-thinking-choosing animals (*logikon zoòn* in Greek). Nevertheless, it would seem that in order to have some sort of connection to current discussion in biology on these issues, Smith employs the concept of "emergence" to explain *that* human personhood *emerging from* its material preconditions or elements could not have been predicted by looking at these elements per se. However, the fact that Smith doesn't explain exactly *how* this emergence occurs leads Vogler to say that "the model of ontological emergentism does a disservice to the strength and power of Smith's account" (an account with which she largely agrees).

Vogler suggests that Smith's account of what makes human personhood irreducible to anything else needs to bracket the question of *how* it emerged in the biosphere and simply take it *as is*, i.e., "[o]n the Thompsonian interpretation . . . the term 'person' becomes a way of marking how things are for an adult human being when all is as it *should be* [italics mine] for an adult human being." This is one of what "Thompson calls 'Aristotelian categoricals' . . . what is not just true about *a* person . . . [but] how things are with *the* person." In other words, Vogler argues that Smith's basically Aristotelian position would be better off if it were formulated in terms of essentialism per se (like Husserl's *Wesenschau*), without any attempt to explain how it *came to be* as such in the biosphere.

Smith and Vogler are self-identified Aristotelians in their acceptance of normative teleology as the key to distinctively or naturally human personhood. Here the continuum of "what is so" and what "ought to be so" is that livings beings *strive to become* what their essential nature attracts them to be. On that fundamental point, Smith and Vogler surely agree. Their difference instead is specific, i.e., it is about the specific advantage or disadvantage of employing "emergentism" for a neo-Aristotelianism entrance into what the French call *les sciences humaines*.

Vogler's Aristotelianism is most evident when she says that "[h]uman society . . . ought to be organized in such a way that each of us can rightly aspire to the higher purposes." Smith's Aristotelianism is most evident when he says "humans have a real end or purpose—a telos . . . to pursue that natural purpose toward flourishing."[2] "Flourishing," a favorite term of neo-Aristotelians (such as Alasdair MacIntyre and John Finnis) is, as Smith notes, an English rendition of "[t]he Greek word . . . *eudaimonia*, which refers to a life objectively well lived . . . leading towards one's telos."[3]

So, my questions directed to both Smith and Vogler are as follows:

1. Do they appropriate Aristotle correctly? Or, have they overlooked (whether intentionally or not) something essential in Aristotle, without which their Aristotelianism is inauthentic?

2. Do they adequately answer the charge of many modern philosophers (for example, Ernst Cassirer, Leo Strauss, and most recently, Jürgen Habermas) that Aristotelian ethics or practical philosophy presupposes that human action fits into a fully teleological universe or cosmos, and since nobody can accept that teleological–cosmological paradigm any more (i.e., after Galileo, Newton, Darwin, Einstein *et alia*), Aristotelian teleological praxis falls with Aristotelian teleological cosmology or even with Aristotelian biology? (Indeed, one might ask Smith whether his embrace of "emergentism" is an attempt to connect to the kind of biology that is partially calling into question the reductionism of the orthodox Darwinians.)

What all of the neo-Aristotelians seem to miss is that Aristotle, when dealing with the ends (*telē*) of human life, which are those actions done for their own sake, is not a pluralist. Despite all the talk of the plurality of virtuous activities, they are not incommensurate. There is only one such activity that resists ever being taken as dependent on or instrumental for something outside itself. That activity is what we would now call "metaphysical" contemplation of God as the *summum bonum*. To be sure, the pursuit of this end cannot be totally exclusive for any embodied human being; even the most contemplative humans still have bodily and political needs, the fulfillment of which is intelligent, purposeful activity. Nevertheless, teleological activity is hierarchal, with only one activity at its apex, an activity done solely for its own sake like the God it intends who acts solely for his own sake. All other good activities (what many neo-Aristotelians, based on an arguable reading of Thomas Aquinas's notion of *bonum faciendum est*, call "goods") only play a secondary role in a human life that is truly *eudaimonic*.

2. Ibid., 400.
3. Ibid., 407.

The role of all these activities is at best a supporting role. As such, Aristotelian practical philosophy is inextricably theological. (One could say the same for Spinoza's practical philosophy.)

However, both Smith and Vogler (whatever their personal religious commitments are) seem to avoid theological questions when stating their respective positions. Vogler talks about "[w]here most *non-theistic* [italics mine] philosophers" want to affirm the distinctiveness of human nature and locate that distinctiveness. She seems to place herself in their camp. But, wouldn't Aristotle say that what makes humans unique (only a little below the heavenly intelligences) is their desire to know God, even though very few humans actually attain that highest level of *eudaimonia*? And Smith is even more direct on this question when he states: "Many thinkers concerned with dignity [i.e., the respect human personhood deserves] do not believe in a dignity-conferring God. . . . [T]hey want an account that is not dependent on belief in God."[4] And, while not placing himself in their camp, Smith seems willing to accommodate himself to John Rawls, Martha Nussbaum, et alia, by suppressing his metaphysical/theological beliefs in order to meet their entrance requirements for secular public discourse.

Nevertheless, we theists, whether Aristotelians or not, can employ our beliefs to give what we think is a better justification of our political positions without requiring nontheists, with whom we can agree on some political positions, to accede to our beliefs. Our metaphysical beliefs *inform* our political positions; but our political positions are not simply *deduced* from them. So, all that need be done along these lines is to show (a là MacIntyre) that everyone has metaphysical beliefs (even if they are anti-metaphysical) despite all protests to the contrary. The question is how human thinkers employ them in public discourse with others having different beliefs.

Finally, though, can one be an Aristotelian theist at all today? For what gives Aristotelian praxis its gravitas is that when one pursues what is good for humans, one is an important, conscious participant in a teleological process that is ubiquitous in the cosmos, and which has ultimacy. Thus the reason that theologians like Maimonides and Aquinas could speak the language of the Aristotelian philosophers was because they both accepted a scientific paradigm of Nature (Aristotle's *ta physika*), which was not only concerned with God, but was concerned with God as the apex of the whole intelligible/intelligent cosmic order.

---

4. Ibid, 400.

Needless to say, that paradigm is irretrievable—at least as far as we now know. If one is to link purposeful human action with concern with God, that concern is not going to be built on the back of natural science (as is Aristotelian ontology); that concern is going to have to be a response to the God who reveals himself in the history of a people (i.e., of *kenesset yisrael*: "the community of Israel," or of the *ekklesia*: "the church"). What would this mean? Discussing human dignity requires that we not suppress our belief that human dignity and human uniqueness comes about because we are the *imago Dei*; which might well mean the human capacity to be reached by God (hence the human desire to be actually reached by God). It will be a new way of speaking to the world, because we have always assumed we were speaking to an essentially Aristotelian audience.

But as a sociologist like Christian Smith knows, any society that attempts to deny the human-God connection is a society that is inhibiting (often violently) human persons from actualizing what makes us unique in the world. Even in the most secular societies, the "God question" just won't go away, but is again and again "the return of the repressed." Human beings may no longer be Aristotelians, but we can still understand them.

Smith, Christian. *What is a Person? Rethinking Humanity, Social Life, and the Moral Good from the Person Up*. Chicago: University of Chicago Press, 2010.

II.5 The Gimlet-Eye of Social Science

James R. Rogers

IN THE PLAY *WIT*, a cancer patient's only hope, and a slim one at that, is to undergo a radical, toxic, experimental treatment. Her attending physician is a research doctor. The results of the experimental treatment interest him more than his patient does. The patient, an English professor who specializes in the use of "wit" in John Donne's poetry, is ignored as a person by her physician, and loses her dignity as a person bit by bit in the clinical interactions she has with various medical technicians and interns. At her death—one made all the more chaotic by confusion over a "do not resuscitate" order—she lies stripped and naked. A medical process with the manifest goal to preserve the person has instead stripped personhood away through neglect and in pursuit of a greater good.

In *What Is A Person?*, Christian Smith argues for a similar irony, the disappearance of "the person" in the study of all things human: the *social* sciences.

> Even the social sciences, for all their sophistication in certain ways, have not helped us much to understand clearly the nature of our own species, humanity as such. Or so I believe. The social sciences are good at describing and analyzing human activities, cultures, institutions, social relations, and social structures. But that is not the same thing as actually understanding humans beings per se, what we are, our constitution and condition. I will argue in the pages that follow that the social sciences have been frequently unhelpful in our search for self-understanding as a particular kind of existent and acting being.[1]

1. Smith, *What is a Person?*, 1.

Smith takes up too many topics to consider in one comment. In my comments, I focus on the limited areas that I engage as a scholar—as an applied game theorist in political science, with some experience with large-N empirical studies.

I divide Smith's argument into two moves. His first move criticizes several main tributaries of scholarship in the social sciences, focusing on his own field of sociology. In his second move he seeks to provide a framework for the practice of a better social science. I first take up Smith's discussion of empirical social science (or "variables" social science), and consider the role of good theory in empirically focused social science. I then consider his criticism of "reductionism" in social science, particularly as applied to rational choice theory, and test his criticism against the subfield of rational choice theory known as "game theory." I argue that Smith's criticisms are largely misplaced, and that rational choice theory done well is consistent with the "personalism" that he champions.

Empiricism

Smith devotes a chapter to what he terms "variables sociology." I understand the "variables" modifier to refer to large-N quantitative studies that typically employ advanced statistical tools, usually econometric in nature. Smith does not reject "variables" social science. Rather,

> When set within a proper theoretical framework for understanding the nature of reality and science (critical realism), and when informed by a proper understanding of human beings (personalism), variables social science can be conducted in theoretically and analytically appropriate and intellectually enlightening ways.[2]

One prominent criticism Smith advances against variables social science is the temptation scholars face to allow the empirical method to dominate the substantive research question. Smith complains, rightly, that poor researchers substitute a search for empirical associations for critical thought and theorizing. Smith laments that theory development—the process that leads to real understanding of social phenomena—suffers as a result of too much emphasis on finding empirical regularities.

> Reality is comprised of a host of entities—material and otherwise—that possess various causal powers and capacities to make

2. Ibid., 279.

things happen in the world. Those powers and capacities are often not empirically observable, at least directly. Also, those capacities are often not always triggered or activated, and so frequently do not operate to influence anything. Yet they exist. . . . A key purpose of social science . . . is not to look for strong correlations between empirical events, but to identify and understand the various underlying causal mechanisms that produce identifiable outcomes and events of interest.[3]

As I understand it, Smith's argument here is a call for empirical studies necessarily to be guided by well-thought-out theory. I couldn't agree more. Indeed, most of the colleagues in my department share Smith's concern, not only in the abstract but concretely in our goals for the department's undergraduate and graduate programs. We regularly discuss our concerns that our doctoral students' focus on mastering empirical methods intellectually crowds out a like development in their theoretical maturity. We discuss how to activate and foster our students' theoretical creativity concomitant with the necessary development of their statistical skills. Perhaps the most damning question at a scholarly talk in my department is, "Now, what's your theory?"

This is not to dismiss empirical studies, whether large-N studies or analytical narratives (a.k.a. theory-driven case studies). But as Smith points out, there is interaction between what is observed and what is unobserved. Limiting one's analysis to the observable often means not being able to understand what one observes.

My colleagues and I would simply think that good science entails theory-driven empirical studies. In the context of Smith's book, I wonder about the relationship between critical realism and good social science. I would certainly grant that good, theory-driven social science research is not inconsistent with critical realism. It is difficult to see, however, that critical realists would produce good social science at rates higher than social scientists equally committed to good science.

But Smith takes an additional step that takes him too far, in my estimation. His criticism does not end with the conclusion that unthinking empiricism begets poor social science. For Smith, the assumptions of quantitative social science are not simply conveniences that allow for research to occur, they imply a whole ontology. In scoring what I think is little more than a debater's point in arguing that "Variables do not make things happen

3. Ibid., 293.

in the social world. Human persons do,"[4] Smith takes the next step to suggest that the outcome of poorly done variables social science is not simply poor science, but that poorly done empirical social science negatively affects its practitioners. I take his discussion to hypothesize that poorly practiced empirical social science has a social impact, leading practitioners to dehumanize the people they study:

> Some may dismiss this matter by insisting that these terms are merely shorthand expressions for what is really more careful but unstated thinking. But sociologists should know better that patterns of speech employed over time in self-governing social groups tend to reify and reinforce as (subjective, observer dependent) "realities" the simpler images suggested by the shorthand rather than the more complicated, accurate thinking of which the better tend to remain aware. So, critical realist personalism asks that the interpretation of statistical results references persons when people are the units of analysis. The difference in how the numbers are interpreted is not trivial. Discourse matters.[5]

Smith makes an important claim here: he explicitly suggests that the rejection of critical realism in social science affects something more than the quality of scientific output. I could counter-assert that my own experience with social scientists, whether I think they are good scientists or not-so-good scientists, leads me to suspect that Smith overclaims his case. But in the name of scholarly humility, I will instead note that Smith here details a theory of how poor social science habits cause social scientists who engage in these habits to dehumanize the subjects of their studies (or as Smith puts it, how they make "Persons disappear"[6]). If appropriate measures could be found, and I think they could be found with a bit of scholarly imagination, then the claim that poorly done empirical social science leads practitioners to dehumanize persons is one worthy of rigorous empirical study. In essence, the question is whether linguistic shortcuts—whether the result of laziness or efficiency—cause social scientists to behave like so many Dr. Kelekians in the play *Wit*. And, further, does it matter to subjects in social science studies as much as in a doctor-patient relationship?

4. Ibid., 289.
5. Ibid., 290.
6. Ibid., 289.

Not All Reductionisms Are Created Equal

Over the course of this argument, Smith makes numerous comments in passing about rational choice theory—almost all of them negative. I want to argue that rational choice theory, and particularly game theory, exemplifies (although it does not exhaust) much of what I take Smith to want in social science theorizing, and where he criticizes it, he's mistaken, mistaking assumptions made for analytical convenience for ontological commitments.

Game theory, as a subset of rational choice theory (at least in the predominant "noncooperative" formulation), provides analytical approach that models strategic interaction between persons. One of the key insights game theoretic analysis regularly motivates is how observed outcomes (a.k.a. "equilibrium outcomes") can critically depend on events that occur with zero probability (i.e., depend on contingencies that are never observed). Or to put it with even a bit more jargon, off-equilibrium play (which is not predicted to be observed) can critically affect the observed, equilibrium path.

One obvious example is the deterrent value of a credible threat. Often times the sanction—whether it be war, prison, a discharged pistol, a poor grade, an impeachment, etc.—is never observed. Yet while *unobserved*, the possibility of the sanction can play an absolutely critical role in shaping the behaviors that are observed. This may seem obvious, yet sometimes that observed behavior is so expected that the strategic context underlying observed behaviors is forgotten. The empirically observed absence of war between the US and the Soviet Union in Europe after World War II came to be considered evidence for large groups of individuals in Europe and the US that the Soviet Union was a peaceful nation and America's deterrent capabilities were simply costly superfluities. (I should add that it was certainly true that pacific intentions on the part of Soviet authorities would also predict the observation of peace. In this case, two theories predicted the same observation. Determining which theory was correct would then require additional theorizing and additional, and perhaps more subtle, empirical observation.)

The essence of rational choice theory is that people respond to incentives in what are often predictable ways. This is not a modern innovation, and one does not need to be committed to a strong version of utilitarianism to hold it. Much of the analysis in the *The Federalist*, for example, is arguments entirely consistent with non-mathematical rational choice theory.

In *Federalist 51*, for example, Madison's invisible-hand theory of how the separation of powers protects liberty against a usurping branch of the US government relies on linking the "personal motives" of an institution's office holders to preserve their own institution's prerogatives. These office holders thereby "resist encroachments" of the other institutions because a political invisible hand, one motivated by the self-interest of the office holders, carves out and protects a space for liberty.

Rational choice theory seeks to refine this notion, not because one must posit that people respond always and only to incentives, but because enough of us do so enough of the time that one can gain significance leverage on many types of behavior by inquiring into the incentive structures the persons inhabit.

The notion of "rationality" in rational choice theory is very thin relative to the popular conception of the term. Rationality basically means that a person can rank alternatives and those rankings are transitive. So if I have a choice between apple, blueberry, and cherry pie, I can rank those choices (which includes being indifferent between two or more choices) and my choices are transitive. So if I prefer apple to blueberry, and blueberry to cherry, then I will also prefer apple to cherry.

This notion of rationality is so thin that even persons that most people would think of as "insane" are perfectly rational for the rational choice theorist: a person can believe himself or herself to be Napoleon, but as long as the person can rank order choices and those choices are transitive, then that person is rational according to rational choice theory. If a person cannot rank choices or if that person's choices are intransitive, it does not challenge the usefulness of the theory, it is just that the theory doesn't apply in those cases. To claim that a theory generates useful insights is not to claim that it generates insights universally.

Smith does advance criticisms even at this basic level, e.g., claiming that the assumption that most rational choice theorists make of preferences being stable across time is unrealistic. Here Smith mistakes a common assumption as being a necessary assumption. It would be straightforward to allow preference to change over time, so long as there is some expected analytical gain from introducing this complication into a model.

Given Smith's broadside against "reductionism," and his criticisms of rational choice theory, I assume that Smith includes the component subfield of game theory within his criticism. Such criticism would be mistaken, particularly for someone with Smith's commitment to critical realism.

After all, game theory sets persons at the center of the theory: one must define the set of "players" as a necessary component of every game. So they exist inescapably in every game. They cannot "disappear" in this framework. When players are institutions rather than people themselves, the modeler typically needs to justify the assumption by appeal to other theories (e.g., the median voter theorem entails that only the preference of the median legislator matters, given certain assumptions, and so "Congress" can be modeled as an individual) or by restricting the preferences of the people in the model to be the same as a representative actor.

So, too, the central idea in game theory (at least for interesting games) is that the players recognize that they are interacting with other players. As in recreational games, the actions that you take are often informed by your assessment of how the other player (or players) will respond. The other player is simultaneously thinking about your play in the same way, knowing full well that your play will depend on your assessment of what I will play and, in turn, what I will play depends on my assessment of how you will respond, etc. This awareness, and the different actions it implies, is what is meant by players being "strategic."

Game theoretic models, no matter how complicated, are nonetheless simple, abstract models of reality. A generic objection to game theoretic models is that they are unrealistic. I agree. But that's their virtue, not their vice, at least when the model is done well.

While simplifying, abstract, and unreal, it is unclear that Smith would consider game-theoretic models to be inherently "reductionistic." On the one hand, he defines reductionism as "some property observed at one level [that] can be fully accounted for and explained by properties, structures, or dynamics operating at a lower level."[7] That does not really apply to game theory, because game structures seek only to specify and formalize relationships; they do not seek to break them down into constituent parts.

Nonetheless, game theory is self-consciously methodologically individualist in its assumptions. Earlier in the book Smith paints methodological individualism as a species of reductionism:

> Note that—contra the view of strong methodological individual-
> ism and atomism—those causal capacities are not present in the
> mere sum total of the parts and cannot be adequately explained by
> reducing the system to its component elements, because the social
> structure is a real emergent product of the *relationality* of parts

---

7. Ibid., 36.

and not simply the features of each part added up. In the end, such emergent social realities can possess immense powers of "downward causation" to influence the consciousness and actions of the individual people from which they emerge—often in ways that may not be consistent with the natural, rational, or even actual interests or desires of many of the people involved. This is because social systems and structures are emergent facts, existent above the individual or personal level, at the higher level of the social.[8]

Smith seems to consider that a commitment to methodological individualism to rule out modeling individuals' interaction with each other with their choices formed and channeled by their environment and the institutions they inhabit. I do not see any inherent inconsistency between methodological individualism and the phenomena that Smith identifies with what he terms "emergent social realities."[9]

For example, the incentive structure of the well-known Prisoners' Dilemma game creates an equilibrium that is both fully consistent with individual rationality and generates outcomes at odds "with the natural, rational, or even actual interests or desires of . . . the people involved."[10] Indeed, the players in the game would *unanimously* choose a *different*, feasible outcome. The provocation of the Prisoners' Dilemma is that it illustrates how individually rational behavior can lead to a socially irrational outcomes. So, too, Nobel Prize-winner Kenneth Arrow's "impossibility theorem" shows that under not particularly strict assumptions, voting by completely rational *individual* voters cannot guarantee *socially* rational outcomes. (This is true even given the very weak notion of rationality employed by rational choice theorists.)

These well-known results lead the late William Riker to argue that political science is the true "dismal science" given the discipline's focus on how and why individually rational behavior so often fails to generate socially optimal or rational outcomes. All of these results that account for "emergent" outcomes are nonetheless also rigorously consistent with methodological individualism. While structures and institutions certainly affect individual behavior—dramatically so—methodological individualism nonetheless requires that the person *not* be forgotten in one's analysis. Smith's sniping at the approach is curious in a book dedicated to finding

8. Ibid., 31.
9. Ibid.
10. Ibid., 36.

the lost person in social science research. I do not see the conflict between Smith's articulation of "emergent reality" and methodological individualism that Smith does.

But whether reductionistic or not, Smith independently criticizes the abstraction of rational choice (and other) theory.

> While many of our social science theories are interesting and do illuminate particular dimensions of human social life, I am not convinced that we as people actually find ourselves well represented by them. When we look at the models of the human operative in, say, exchange theory, social control theory, rational choice, functionalism, network theory, evolutionary theory, sociobiology, or sociological Marxism, we may recognize certain aspects of our lives in them. Otherwise the theories would feel completely alien and implausible to us. But I suspect that few of us recognize in those theories what we understand to be most important about our own selves as people. Something about them fails to capture our deep subjective experience as persons, crucial dimensions of the richness of our own lived lives, what thinkers in previous ages might have called our "souls" or "hearts." That itself is not a fatal flaw for such theories. But it does raise questions about such an apparent mismatch between scholarly theory and personal experience.
>
> I think that when social scientists work with professional theoretical depictions of the human that are at odds with their personal, moral, and political views of the human, something else unintentional is going on: the influence of a powerful background assumption about social science—namely, the model of naturalistic positivist empiricism that demands that the social sciences emulate the natural sciences.[11]

Later Smith discusses how "Personalism . . . rejects the human image constructed and promoted by individualistic liberalism, libertarianism, social contractarianism, rational choice theory, and exchange theory."[12]

Well, I can't speak to all of the other theories or approaches that Smith includes in his lists of defective theories. But I can speak to rational choice theory, most specifically as applied in game theory. And Smith has it wrong, conflating assumptions made for analytical convenience with commitments to ontologies.

11. Ibid., 2–4.
12. Ibid., 67.

As we will see, abstraction can be poorly done. But it can also be useful. No theory, including Christian Smith's theory, really aims to replicate reality. Indeed, if one wants reality in all its complexity, then all one needs to do is look out the window. The point of analysis is to understand reality, and humans do that inescapably, whether using words, pictures and illustrations, or mathematical symbols. The unrealism of game theoretic models—or of any model, for that matter—is not a vice, it is a virtue. As with any abstraction (whether prosaic, mathematical, graphical or some combination), the value of the abstraction hinges on the model's usefulness. The very unrealism of a model, if properly constructed, is what makes it useful.

Let's consider a different topic. Rather than "What is a Person?," let us consider a scholar who wrote a book called *What is a Place?* The author rails against the unrealism and abstraction of maps; they simply do not do justice to what "place" truly is. And, indeed, it is obvious that street maps are highly abstracted representations of the real topography of a city. Maps distort what is *really* there and leave out hosts of details about what a particular area looks like. But it is precisely *because* the map distorts reality—because it abstracts away from a host of details of what is really there—that it becomes useful. A map that attempts to portray the full details of a particular area would be too cluttered to be useful in finding a particular location or too large to be stored in a glove compartment. So it is with the game-theoretic models. They seek to abstract away from a host of details that are not relevant to the phenomenon under study. It is the very abstraction that permits us analytically to hold everything else equal and to focus on the most salient aspects of the phenomenon.

Of course, everything is not always equal and omitted details can matter. Just as with street maps, there can be better models and worse models for particular purposes. Maps that abstract away from too much detail won't be useful in finding a particular street or address. Models that abstract away from too much pertinent detail aren't useful for understanding the phenomenon being studied. The trick, then—which is as much a matter of aesthetic taste as it is intellectual judgment—is to develop models that provide just enough detail to be useful for their intended purpose without being so complex that they confuse rather than illuminate. Further, maps can be initially off-putting abstractions from reality for those unfamiliar with them. Many maps use specialized symbols and representations that require some time and effort to learn.

If the author of *What is a Place?* were to object that the map really doesn't help us to understand the true being of a place, most of us would respond with the obvious retort that it's not supposed to. No one conflates the assumptions necessary to generate a useful map with some sort of commitment to the ontology of place. If the author criticizes the map, arguing that it is too reductionistic to be useful, the appropriate response is to invite the author to generate a more complex map and to demonstrate its superiority in assisting us with our task. To this question I now turn.

Smith's Contribution to Doing Social Science: The Proof of the Pudding

Smith time and again posits the need for more robust theories of the human person in order to generate good social science.

> When it comes to the human, therefore, reductionist moves toward either the physical or the mental, the material or the idea, the corporeal or the spiritual are unacceptable and self-defeating. Humans are embodied souls who can only be well understood and explained in light of that complex reality.[13]

As the editor of a journal dedicated to developing political science theory, I often receive manuscripts laying out a new "framework for analysis" that the author purports will explain a set of political phenomena better than the extant alternatives. I am entirely willing to believe the author's claims about the power of the new framework. Nonetheless, I provide a desk rejection to each one. I quite sincerely invite the author to take the new framework and apply it to a specific puzzle that animated the previous scholarship that the author found limited or defective, and that prompted the development of the new framework. Then write that paper and submit it to my journal.

By doing so, the author could demonstrate, rather than assert, the value of the new framework in solving the intellectual puzzles that motivated the previous research and, presumably, motivated the author to articulate the new framework. I am earnest in my invitation. But I have not yet received one of those articles back in that form.

I am not a sociologist. Perhaps trained sociologists could take the frame of "critical realism" as Smith explains it in his book, and deduce a concrete way of studying sociology differently and better than they do

13. Ibid., 22.

now. Smith invites scholars to consider persons as the complex persons we truly are. In my scholarly world, every bit of additional complexity normally reduces my ability to understand the causal world that humans inhabit as persons. Even on Smith's terms, increased complexity carries with it increased opportunity cost for the scholar. Therefore, complexity needs to be justified by the promise of increased insight in the results of the study. Specifically, a more complex theory is justified only when it provides greater understanding of human behavior or social outcomes. Without that promise, there is no need for the increased complexity. The one question with which I came away from Smith's book was this: what puzzles in the discipline of sociology can you solve better than the extant theories, and can you show your framework solves better than the extant theories? The answer is not obvious to me. But I remain entirely open to evidence.

Smith, Christian. *What is a Person? Rethinking Humanity, Social Life, and the Moral Good from the Person Up.* Chicago: University of Chicago Press, 2010.

II.6 Reductive Temptations

Stephen C. Meredith

As Stan Laurel's wife tells him in *Sons of the Desert*, honest confession is good for the soul, so here is a full disclosure: I am an arch-reductionist. Soften the blow a little: a part-time arch-reductionist. Furthermore, I am not a sociologist or a social scientist at all. My day job is to study the structure of aggregating proteins that are involved in neurodegenerative diseases such as Alzheimer's disease. For this work, I use a technique called nuclear magnetic resonance (NMR) spectroscopy, which has to do with spin dynamics. (Spin is a quantum mechanical property; mathematics aside, no one can quite say what spin is.) I have no business commenting on Christian Smith's new book, *What is a Person?*, nor in responding to James Rogers's comments about this book. This little confession is not entirely irrelevant.

I will respond, as I must, as a biochemist trespassing into social science. The central concept in Professor Smith's outstanding, compendious new book (if I may be permitted this one bit of evaluation) is *emergence*, of which he gives many examples. The most important of these, surely, is the emergence of the person above and beyond the welter of scientific data from chemistry, biology, psychology, sociology, and yes, even quantum mechanics. I too will refrain from commenting on most of the twists and turns of this book, focusing instead on two central and complementary questions that run throughout both the book and Professor Rogers's comments. The first is: why would anyone engage in reductionism since, as Professor Smith has it, in doing so one runs the risk of missing the person-forest for all the empirical data-trees? The second is: why would anyone not engage in reductionism since, as Smith acknowledges and Rogers emphasizes, some reduction of a system's complexity may at times be necessary in order to gain rational understanding of the system?

II.6 Reductive Temptations

To reduce, or not to reduce. Is reductionism (always) a necessity for delimiting the field of inquiry so that knowledge is possible? Or, on the other hand, is it (always) a path to our dangerous, intellectually lazy tendency to make unjustified ontological commitments to only those things that our senses can sense—as the old joke has it, always looking under the lamppost because that's where the light is. Yes, to both, of course—albeit in different ways.

If truth, as Thomas Aquinas said, is the adequation of the mind to reality, then anyone with an ounce of horse sense, let alone with even a trace of knowledge about scientific history, ought give up, eternally, on learning Truth, capital T. We can no more apprehend Truth than we can see God with our natural eyes. But we press onward, nevertheless. We can, if we are extremely fortunate, solve an intellectual problem that presses upon us . . . but there is a catch. I believe in atoms and quantum mechanics as fully as I believe in the existence of the island of Tasmania, despite never having seen either one. While I might see Tasmania some day, I will never see an atom; and yet, my observations of them in NMR spectroscopy are so thoroughly theory-laden that I could never plausibly not see them. Our theories are necessary for us to see, and this is as true for quantum physics (and, I assume, for sociology), as it was also for the Apostle Thomas. We must reduce, therefore, because we require theories in order to see; and reduction is born of theories of where to look for truth.

But, on the other hand, perhaps Professor Smith has alerted us to a real danger. As Rogers put it, summarizing Smith: "Smith . . . suggest[s] that the outcome of poorly done variables social science is not simply poor science, but that poorly done empirical social science negatively affects its practitioners. I take his discussion to hypothesize that poorly practiced empirical social science has a social impact, it leads practitioners to dehumanize the people they study." But, as Rogers argues, Smith goes even further. At issue is whether it is *only* bad social (or biological) science that does this; or, on the other hand, is it possible that empirical science, even done well, carries this danger with it? We would not endorse anarchy because of the existence of bad governments, or forswear chemistry because of the phlogiston theory. Science, properly done, has a self-correcting side to it: bad theories, including ones in sociology or biology that dehumanize the person, will collapse under their own weight, as the phlogiston theory did in chemistry. And thus, Rogers imagines, somewhat wistfully, how "the claim that poorly-done empirical social science leads practitioners to dehumanize persons" might itself be "worthy of rigorous empirical study."

Rogers's point about bad science is a fair one, and one on which he and Smith might agree: that bad science is more corrupting of our concept of the human person than good science—"bad" and "good" referring not only to the quality of the empirical data, but also to the qualities, including the moral qualities, of the theories behind the data. And Professor Smith is careful, throughout his book, to avoid any simple anti-empirical stance. There is still a place, in sociology and biology, as there is in quantum mechanics, for good empirical data.

The issue remains, however, whether even the best social scientist is corrupted by focusing too doggedly on the empirical data. I don't know the answer to this question, but I will offer a few thoughts from my own field. To paraphrase something Leon Kass said, good intellect is no guarantee of good character. Even brilliant scientists may be bad people. The parallel problem in the biological sciences to the one described by Professor Smith in the social sciences, I would say, is to see persons merely as collections of cells—or proteins, atoms, or quarks. Which they *are*; but the problem is the word "merely," "only," or, as Professor Smith put it, "nothing but-tery." I will add one more, which I have heard more times than I would have wished: "A brain is a collection of neurons. Period." Wherefore "period"? I am enough of a contrarian that among other scientists I sometimes raise the question of the soul, knowing that it will drive certain types of biological scientists into a rage.

And so I ask this question: why should a biological scientist *not* believe in the soul, if the soul is not some vague and misty thing, as Hume thought it to be, but rather, as Thomas Aquinas wrote, the first principle of things that live, i.e., the form of the living body? Similarly, why should the neuroscientist, studying central neurons, not also have a concept of *mind* as the form of the functioning *brain*? Wherefore "period," indeed!

Professor Rogers argues that "Not All Reductionisms Are Created Equal," and one must agree. He also laments the fact that among some students, the "focus on mastering empirical methods intellectually crowds out a like development in their theoretical maturity." In view of my earlier statements that we cannot see anything without a theory of what we're looking at, I agree that this is a serious problem too. But while avoiding "nothing but-tery" might be possible, we must also ask why it happens that people can succumb to it, even while doing *exemplary* empirical research.

To avoid this fate requires both intellectual modesty and tireless probity and self-scrutiny, and these are too often scant in universities. But it may be something else as well.

In 1907, Dr. Duncan MacDougall of Haverhill, Massachusetts proposed to measure the weight of the human soul. His "experiment" consisted of having patients with tuberculosis lie on a bed that had been suspended, in turn, on a large but supposedly sensitive and accurate scale. When the patient died, the soul would leave his body, and the decrease in weight would be the weight of the human soul, which he famously (or infamously) declared to be twenty-one g. The science was bad . . . really bad, and he was lambasted in the press for his bad science.

In my opinion, however, bad science was the least of his problems. His main problem was philosophical. There is a serious category error in his gratuitous assumption that the soul is a body—which it is not, and *cannot* be. (As Thomas Aquinas said, if the soul were a body, then all bodies could be souls, even dead ones; a living body must be *"sic,"* such a body, not just a body *simpliciter*.) But beyond this error, the question we should ask ourselves is why this man, even in the service of a religious doctrine, should be eager to determine the *weight* of the soul. The prestige of empirical science weighed upon the religious thought of this physician—contaminated it, as it were, even though it was none too pure before it got contaminated. It may be true, as Rogers says, that even while practicing empirical science, it is not necessary to become a slave to empirical data. But the temptation is ubiquitous, and Professor Smith's book stands as a good warning to us all.

II.7 Reply to My Critics

Christian Smith

I AM GRATEFUL FOR the thoughtful responses to my book, *What is a Person?* We are dealing here with crucial issues involving the bases of both good social scientific scholarship and good societies, so it is important that we think carefully, to do our best to get it right.

In what follows, I focus the majority of my response on James Rogers's questions about my book, exploring the issues of reductionism and complexity in social science, as they relate to differences between Rogers's rational-choice–game-theory approach and my own critical realist personalism. But all that follows concerns the larger issue of what human persons are and how our assumptions about person shape social science.

On Reductionism

One of the most important issues in my book and in the responses to it is *reductionism*. What exactly do we mean by that idea, by someone being reductionistic? Are there kinds of reductionism that might be valuable or even necessary? In my book, I defined reductionism as "trying to understand certain entities by reducing them to their component parts existing at lower levels."[1] I then clarified that as follows:

> It is crucial here to distinguish *reductionism* from *reduction*. I am not here opposing *methodological* reduction (the partial decomposition of elements at one level into parts at a different level for purposes of systematic analysis) per se, which is an essential aspect of science when appropriately done; my argument rather contradicts

1. Smith, *What is a Person?*, 28.

both *ontological* reductionism, which fails to acknowledge and understand the complexly stratified nature of reality, and *causal* reductionism, which routinely seeks to explain facts and events by more basic features and causes operating at lower levels.[2]

Despite my careful clarification, it seems we still need to clarify what we do and do not mean by "reductionism." Some of my respondents discuss "reductionism" in ways reflecting meanings that are different from mine. Consequently, the discussion here has run with at least two and possibly three distinct meanings being assigned to one term. No wonder we do not agree on whether reductionism is a good or bad or necessary or avoidable practice.

In contrast to my defined meaning of reductionism, James Rogers has slipped into the discussion another, different meaning for the term. That is the idea that every scientific theory and analytical perspective inevitably oversimplifies reality in order to make it cognitively tractable. The example of this he defends is game theory and the rational-choice assumptions that underwrite it. In Rogers's world, such "reductionism" offers necessary "analytical convenience" and so is useful precisely because it "distorts reality" and is "unrealistic." Rogers also suggests maps as examples of reality-simplifying models that help us get valuable work done (find our way in some terrain) even at the inevitable cost of distorting aspects of reality that "are not relevant to the phenomenon under study." Hence, he suggests, reductionism is not only legitimate but essential to the task of science.

That much is correct. All of science works with simplified models of reality. But Rogers is confused and confusing in his equating that practice with reductionism. In critical realist terms, what he is describing is not reductionism but "abstraction" and "conceptualization." Yes, every science abstracts certain crucial aspects of the massive complexity of life on which it focuses. And, yes, all scientific attempts to understand and explain reality require sets of concepts that together theoretically model some aspect of the world in a way that makes it amenable to human comprehension. "All theoretical knowledge of reality is conceptually mediated," critical realists say (though embodied, "practical" knowledge may not be). Abstraction and conceptualization lie at the heart of the critical realist program of social analysis.

But, to return to the issue at hand, this kind of necessary theoretical abstraction and conceptualization is *an entirely different matter* from reductionism as I have critiqued it. Rogers almost recognizes that difference

2. Ibid.

when he notes that it is unclear whether I would consider game theory models to be inherently reductionistic. Then the distinction disappears in his discussion and he goes on to defend reductionism as necessary in the name of theoretical abstraction and conceptualization. But conflating these terms badly confuses the discussion. It also creates an opening for pernicious reductionism to slip into our scholarship. When we highlight the distinctions between the two different meanings, we see that we can absolutely embrace abstraction and conceptualization as essential to science, while rejecting reductionism (as I have defined it) as wrong and destructive.

How easily these two distinct ideas can become conflated is evident in Stephen Meredith's piece, where he says we "must agree" with Rogers's contention that "not all reductionisms are created equal." (The plural form, reductionisms, indicates that, again, we confusingly have more than one meaning of our single term running in this discussion.) Meredith seems to concede that "reductionism" constitutes the heart of scientific theorizing: "We must reduce . . . because we require theories in order to see; and reduction is borne of theories of where to look for truth." He thus associates reductionism with "theoretical maturity."

But, again, Meredith here is repeating Rogers's confusion of two distinct issues: reductionism, on the one hand (bad), and theoretical abstraction and conceptualization, on the other hand (good and necessary). Without this distinction clearly in view, again, "nothing but-tery" sneaks in the back door of science under the benign guise of theoretical abstraction, but with consequences that are pernicious. Having collapsed this distinction, Meredith obviously feels uncomfortably caught on a fence, pulled on the one side by the logic of, in his words, "why would anyone engage in reductionism?" and on the other by the question, "why would anyone *not* engage in reductionism?"

But those are not two sides of one fence. Meredith is wrestling with a false dilemma. These are completely different matters. One has to do with the mental operations involved in all human theoretical knowing—abstracting out of all of the possible features of reality the most important features—in order to highlight them as the most important for understanding and explaining something of particular interest. The other is about insisting that everything concerning some aspect of some entity existing at one level of reality can be fully accounted for and explained by some lower, less complex level of that same reality (e.g., human persons are "nothing but" their brains and bodies, which are "nothing but" bits of matter and energy transfers, ad nauseam). In short, we can and must reject pernicious tendencies in science toward reductionism without compromising the abstraction and conceptualization needed to construct our theories.

On Persons in Rational Choice Theory

Having clarified that, we need next to critically consider a few related matters. One concerns Rogers's claim that "game theory sets persons at the center." This is correct, sort of. One of the few virtues of rational choice theory is that it is explicit about its assumptions concerning human nature, in contrast to many social science theories, which often fudge the issue. The main problem with the rational choice approach, however, is that its explicit view of human nature is ultimately *wrong*, in being misleadingly incomplete. Yes, people tend to act strategically in responding to incentives. But that assumption captures only one among many important dimensions of human consciousness, life, and action. The reality is immensely more complex. This is why, in order to protect the rational-choice paradigm against reality, its advocates have needed to thin the theory out. The utilitarian roots of the approach are said to be able to be cut off and discarded, for example. People are said to be predictable only "given their preferences." And so on.

In the end, on the matter of human personhood, *rational choice theory must be finally either tautological or false.* To prevent it from being empirically false, it has to be watered down to something like "people generally try to do what they actually think they should do, to the extent that they can." But that is not very impressive. It is essentially tautological: people do what they think they should do and the way we know this is because that is what they generally do.

To prevent rational choice theory from being tautological, its theoretical claims must be tightened up, advancing stronger assumptions about valued ends, rationality, and deliberation. And these turn out to be empirically false, in light of the complexities of real human life. Rational choice may prove useful as an approach to explain human behavior in well-defined markets with shared understandings of metrics and values. But if we want to understand and explain real human personhood, action, and social life, rational choice theory is not a very good place to start or end. From a realist's view, that is because its basic assumptions are abstract, conceptual, and simpler than reality itself. They are also grossly simplistic and fatally incomplete, and so fundamentally misleading.

On Adequate Complexity

At this point, Rogers will no doubt wish to fall back upon his argument about all scientific analyses needing to oversimplify reality for the sake of "usefulness." This will not do. Any approach that is prepared to sacrifice reality for the sake of "analytical usefulness" must explain what even counts as "useful" and why that and not something else should count and trump other goods.

Rogers does not specify what he means by "usefulness."

The philosophical name for Rogers's view that a scientific theory is good if it is "useful" (setting aside the question of what counts as useful) is known as theoretical "instrumentalism." In this view, theories do not represent reality. They are mental instruments that help us get something done that we want done. The theory may be bunk as far as reality is concerned, but if it is "useful," then it is good. Such a view adopts the anti-ontological sensibility of American pragmatism, namely, that we should drop the concern to understand the way things really are and focus instead on solving our immediate practical problems, however we define them.

By contrast, critical realism insists that our theories and explanations be *realistic*, that they represent features of reality as accurately as possible. That does not mean they need to fully capture every aspect of reality at once, which is impossible. But it rejects making ideas central that openly admit to being "unrealistic." That violates the basic task of science, which is to tell us what exists in reality and how it works to produce or prevent important outcomes and conditions of interest.

The real point of theoretical simplification is to highlight key causal processes at work in social life, not to distort and falsify reality. Highlighting crucial parts of reality to emphasize does not make claims about them that are "unrealistic." And in all of this, good science normally pushes strongly in the direction of having to figure out how to model greater complexity. The critical realist watchword, therefore, is, "Get ready for some real complexity." Rational choice theory, however, ignores and resists most of the complexities of reality, preferring to compact reality into something more manageable.

Nonetheless, Rogers commends to us "just enough detail to be useful for . . . intended purposes without being so complex as to confuse rather than illuminate." Again, what counts as "illuminating" and why? At what point do we become "confused" and why there? And how are our "intended purposes" even determined in the first place, and on what basis? Consider: what if what reality had to tell us first and foremost is that reality is more complex than any of our social sciences can really understand and explain well? How could Rogers's approach ever learn that lesson from reality? What if what *we* found "illuminating" was not very important?

Rogers says that "a more complex theory is justified only when it provides greater understanding of human behavior or social outcomes." Okay, good. Given the massively complex nature of every aspect of real human life, by that standard, more complex theories will nearly always be justified. Greater complexity will—even as implied by Rogers's own previous argument about the need to simplify reality—model our complex reality better. So then why does Rogers resist added complexity? He writes that, "in my scholarly world, every bit of additional complexity normally reduces my ability to understand the causal world that humans inhabit as persons." But we don't learn from this statement that there is something wrong with the adequate-complexity-demanding critical realist view of science. Rather, there is something wrong with Rogers's "scholarly world."

The problem of course is not James Rogers himself, but the larger institutional and theoretical paradigm to which he is committed. This problem is also evident in his concern that added complexity presents an "increased opportunity cost for the scholar." Such a view is badly out of whack. Critical realism says that we scientists must be prepared to pay the necessary costs to understand the contents of reality as they are and how they work. To think, per Rogers, that reality has to adjust itself to fit *our* models and procedures, in order that the costs of *our* scholarship may be reduced, is a travesty.

Additional Problems

The problems in Rogers's account run wider and perhaps deeper. For example, he seems confident that the social scientist can know which of the myriad factors operating in human social life are "not relevant to the phenomenon under study," such that they can be bracketed away as extraneous. That is at least sometimes doubtful. Certain important factors are commonly considered irrelevant by scholars as a matter of their a priori presupposition, not on the basis of open-eyed empirical evidence, so that presumed "useful" analytical paradigms end up excluding certain factors from study before they can even be considered.

Think, for example, of the power of religion to shape human social life. For much of the twentieth century, religion was ignored in US higher education, due to the "commonsense obviousness" of secularization theory to academics at the time. Or think of people's truly irrational behavior, including consumer and financial behavior, in which most of us recurrently engage. A great deal of systematic research, including in behavioral economics, not to mention a simple observation of world history, has shown that humans are often only marginally rational in many of their perceptions, choices, and dealings. What earlier modern thinkers called "the passions" play a major role in human personal and social life. Yet the force of such passions, irrational choice, and institutional power that govern much human action is axiomatically excluded from analytical view by many standard, inherited economic theories.

On the flip side, Rogers seems confident about our ability to know "the most salient aspects of the phenomenon," and seems comfortable with the idea of "holding everything else equal" in our analyses. On the first point, I must ask again: how do we actually know which parts of reality are "most salient"? And how confident should we be in that knowledge? All too often our theoretical paradigms answer these questions, not reality itself. Academic science thus too readily constructs "reality," rather than allowing reality to determine its findings. On the second point, the very idea of "holding everything else equal"—a notion ingrained in quantitative social science—also reflects a readiness to sacrifice reality as it is for the sake of grossly oversimplified models and publishable findings. Ceteris paribus may work well in mind experiments. But as a method for describing and explaining the terrain of the real world, it usually operates as an out-of-control, landscape-razing bulldozer.

Consider too a problem that the role of "preferences" in rational choice and game theory creates. If people's preferences are the determinants of their transitive rankings and choices, then should we not be focusing our attention on the sources and nature of people's preferences rather than the situational choices they make? Even by Rogers's assumptions, preferences are where the action is, and preferences are mostly cultural (as well as naturally embodied in biology). So shouldn't social scientists, including economists, be studying culture more than value-maximizing, situational choices? If Rogers is correct, then what he and his kind are spending most of their time observing is relatively trivial. If we presuppose with Rogers that people respond rationally to their incentives, why is it useful to show empirically that people respond to incentives? Much more important, it seems to me, would be showing what kinds of cultural beliefs tend to order people's cognitive assumptions and perceptions.

Ponder too some other tensions embedded in game theory. It claims allegiance to methodological individualism. But it also focuses explanations on the incentives that individuals face. So the actual choices individuals make turn out to be nearly inevitable, predictable, given the incentives encountered. Thus, Rogers may say that human persons play a central role in game theory, but in reality "persons" in his game are little more than perceiving-and-choosing–calculators-of-gain. The real determinants of action are the incentives, not the persons, which is why sophisticated game-theory models can be simulated on computers instead of having to be based on actual observational data.

At the same time, rational-choice game-theory scholars tend to ignore the fact that the game itself represents a *real social structure*. Such scholars will talk about "incentive structures," but typically view them as variable, manipulable, and transitory. In real human social and institutional life, however, incentive structures are usually embedded in and presented by durable social structures that are as real as our bodies and our minds. Acknowledging this genuine reality of social structures has the unfortunate consequence for methodological individualists of undercutting their belief that, for purposes of social explanation, what really matters are the aggregate choices and activities of individual persons.

Well, no. The social structures that contain individuals matter as much as the actions of individuals themselves. Critical realist personalism is able to coherently explain why it is necessary to account both for personal actors and social structures in any social science explanation and how that might be done. What puzzles in sociology, Rogers asks, can my critical realist personalism solve better than the extant theories? Immodestly, I say: all of them. But that must begin by first allowing critical realism to call into question the established what's, why's, and how's of what it even means to successfully "solve a puzzle" in the social sciences.

Much of normal social science today deserves to collapse under the weight of the myriad anomalies and inadequacies that beset it. So I am not merely proposing to do normal science in a marginally more "useful" way, by proposing a "new framework of analysis." The philosophy of critical realism and the view of human beings advanced by personalism demand some major changes in the taken-for-granted assumptions, standards, and practices of social science today. Were that to happen, Rogers might better appreciate the demonstrably productive tool that critical realist personalism is and offers.

Explaining the Difference

Some readers might say that the differences between Rogers and me simply reflect the disciplinary divergences between economics and sociology. "Economics," it has aptly been said, "is about the rational basis for seemingly irrational behavior, while sociology is about the irrational and a-rational basis of seemingly rational behavior." There is something to that.

But I think that explanation is too shallow. What is finally at issue here is a fundamental difference in philosophies of social science. Rogers' rational-choice, game-theory approach is informed broadly by a kind of positivist empiricism. Its assumptions about human beings are clearly drawn from a rationalist and broadly utilitarian stream of thought. Rogers also operates with an instrumentalist view of the purpose of theory in the scientific enterprise.

I approach the task of social science guided by the philosophy of critical realism, my views of human beings reflect the tradition of personalism, and I reject theoretical instrumentalism in favor of theoretical realism. Governed by our divergent governing philosophical frameworks, we differ on many specific points. But my larger point is that *my framework is better than his.*

In the 1990s, a decade in the academy much influenced by the cognitive relativism of the then ascendant postmodernism, many would have thrown up their hands and said, "To each tribe its own local narrative!" "Celebrate incoherent diversity!" and "It's all about perspective and who is to judge which is better?" Thankfully, reality and realism have since helped to pull us out of that intellectual abyss. Indeed, the very fact that we are even having these discussions reflects a deeper agreement that rational argumentation and solid evidence hold the potential to adjudicate disagreeing views, as difficult as that may be. My hope in writing this response to Rogers is to cast some doubt on the adequacy of his working paradigm and to add reasons to believe in the greater realism, coherence, and explanatory adequacy of critical realist personalism.

On Ontological Emergence

Candace Vogler and I are, I believe, on the same page in thinking about human persons, despite what her response to my book might suggest otherwise. Sorting it all out would take more words that I have left, but a few clarifications should make much clear.

First, and most importantly, I think Vogler has misunderstood my approach as depending on methodological individualism. In fact, critical realism absolutely rejects methodological individualism. My commitment to this position is not "unacknowledged." I am against it. My account does not try to understand persons "solely on the basis of their properties." The whole idea of ontological emergence, in fact, is that the interaction or relation of entities at one level of reality brings into existence entities with features, properties, and powers that are *not found* at the lower level. So she and I agree that methodological individualism is not the way to go. But I remain convinced that ontological emergence is needed to show how parts and wholes work together in one coherent reality.

Vogler encourages me to begin directly from the whole, using something like Michael Thompson's Aristotelian account of humans and their nature. I am friendly to that idea. In fact, that is what I think I actually do in my book, beginning with my first claims about the ontological reality of persons. I begin establishing the fact of persons who are irreducible to any capacities, features, powers, or parts at the sub-personal level. Having made that point, I only then go "down" a level to human capacities and powers and work back upwardly through ontological emergence to show how the fact of integral personhood fits within a larger dynamic of a single yet complex and differentiated reality. We thus see that persons are not merely composed of parts but, due to emergence, are qualitatively much more than those parts.

The point is to make sense of the idea that persons can emerge out of their subcomponents yet not be reducible to them, while showing how that is not radically different from how the rest of reality is put together. But that, I think, is simply viewing the same coherent fact from two different perspectives, the Thompsonian Aristotelian view and the upwardly moving view of ontological emergence. And the latter does not preclude the former. In my mind, it simply adds an extremely helpful explanation for how the whole of the person is related to the lower-order parts from which persons emerge.

Now, what is absolutely true is that what happens in ontological emergence is sometimes *mysterious*. And I have no doubt that philosophers have no idea how to do the work to fully explain ontological emergence. That simply may never be possible. But that itself does *not* mean that emergence does not happen, is not real, does not provide the best way to think about how reality is put together. It just means that we humans have limits to our ability to understand and explain the details of how everything works. But so what? The same is true of gravity. We must take what we can get in understanding, as our "best account," and try to improve it as we can. Meanwhile, reality does not depend on philosophers being able to spell out the details. It is what it is, whatever it is, and however "slippery" it may feel to us at any time.

I am absolutely convinced, along with all other critical realists and many other thinkers, that reality involves strong ontological emergence in its basic makeup and operation. I do not believe that science or philosophy will ever solve the "epistemological" problems in a way that will eliminate the need for emergence as a concept. And, meanwhile, I think ontological emergence itself solves many problems we face, even if it requires us to admit a crucially mysterious dimension to reality.

Having said that, however, I think two other key clarifications are in order. Vogler seems to define emergence (or says others define it) as concerning whether we can or cannot "predict" features and properties of the emergent state from the state of the preemergent entities. David Novak adopts the same definition. But the ability to predict emergent properties and powers from knowledge of the preemergent ones is *not* what matters, in the critical realist view. Prediction is not the issue. At issue instead is whether the emergent properties and powers are present among the preemergent entities from which the emergent entity emerged. In cases of true emergence, they cannot be found there.

Vogler also describes emergence as involving conditions where the allegedly emergent entities do not have the features or obey the laws operative of the preemergent state. But my view reverses that equation. What matters in emergence involves conditions where *the preemergent entities* do not have the features, powers, or tendencies that are operative in the emergent entities.

These differences of understanding of emergence may explain why some philosophers remain suspicious of ontological emergence while others of us find emergence to be intuitively obvious. Further inquiry into agreement and disagreement on the points that Vogler raises, therefore, should probably begin with a more precise accounting of definitions and meanings of key terms. For now, however, I can say that while I greatly appreciate her attempt to strengthen my case by suggesting that I be more cautious, I will stick with my bolder ontological approach.

On the Theological Meaning of Persons

Phillip Cary's essay on the historical rootedness in theological debates of our cultural understandings of human beings as "persons" is very fine. I agree with it almost entirely. David Yeago's commentary on Cary's essay is equally insightful and appreciated. I take no issue with either. I would here only underscore two points important to my argument, both of which I believe Cary and Yeago understand and may affirm, but which are worth reiterating in this context.

The first is that we must not confuse historically developing cultural understandings of a reality with the ontological reality itself. The widespread influence of "social constructionism" in academia and our culture might suggest that human beings really are not persons as a matter of ontological reality, but that we have only come contingently to think of them as persons in our context, given our particular history. Some might similarly suggest that human beings were not persons before we constructed the category of persons, but that the self-creative, self-reflexivity of human beings about their own personhood eventually turned us into persons. In either case, human beings per se are not really ontologically persons as a matter of reality. Rather, our (alleged) personhood is merely an accidental idea about ourselves.

I believe and argue in my book that such a view is wrong. I am quite sure that Cary and Yeago also agree with me on that. Critical realist personalism argues that all human beings are and have been (at least since the Axial Age) persons as I describe personhood, whether or not any given person or culture recognized or had the theoretical language to name that fact. The real personhood of all living human beings as an ontological fact, whether or not any person or culture recognized it, is similar in this way to the real existence of germs as the cause of many sicknesses and diseases, even though for most of human history people knew little to nothing about germs. The eventual recognition and knowledge about germs did not bring them into ontological being. Rather, cultural-developmental responses of recognition and knowledge brought to light the always-existent ontological reality of germs. What Cary's essay shows us is not that theology "invented" the reality of personhood, but instead that problems in Christian theology provided the historical means by which humanity has come to recognize its own ontologically real personhood.

Second, as both Cary and Yeago correctly point out, yes, a definite tension does exist in my account of personhood and the religious grounding of the belief in human dignity that comes with the personhood of human beings. I address this tension explicitly in my book. And yes, it does mean that my personalist project "faces enormous difficulties," as Yeago warns. Yet even from a confessional perspective of religious faith, if human personhood is indeed an ontological fact of reality and not a social construction, then that itself should create the basis for people of faith to constructively engage nonreligious and secular people, and even agnostics and atheists, on the question of personhood. For if human personhood is indeed a real fact of our shared humanity, whether we are religious or not, it still ought to create a sturdy bridge between one understanding of our human condition and another. Here is how I said this in the book:

> I am interested in a defensible account of dignity that bridges across as many people of good will as possible, one that includes as many discussion partners as it is able who believe in and want to protect human dignity. I think that if a good theistic account of human dignity is valid, we should expect the truth it explains on the human side of the divine-human relationship to show up and be discernable in lived human life. Human dignity, even if its ultimate source is in God, should disclose itself in various this-worldly experiences, signs, and evidences that even people who do not believe in God may observe and about which they may rationally theorize.[3]

While I am recurrently tempted to despair over the prospects of civil, rational, constructive argumentation about and advance in social theory in the academy, I find in the end that I am not allowed to despair. So I continue to champion critical realist personalism.

Smith, Christian. *What is a Person? Rethinking Humanity, Social Life, and the Moral Good from the Person Up.* Chicago: University of Chicago Press, 2010.

3. Ibid.

Bibliography

Austin, Norman. *Archery at the Dark of the Moon.* Los Angeles: University of California Press, 1975.

Aquinas, Thomas. *Summa Theologica.* 5 vols. Translated by the Fathers of the English Dominican Province. Notre Dame, IN: Christian Classics, 1948.

Bellah, Robert. *Religion in Human Evolution: From the Paleolithic to the Axial Age.* Cambridge, MA: Harvard University Press, 2011.

Chesterton, G.K. "The Catholic Church and Conversion." In *The Collected Works of G.K. Chesterton,* vol. 3, 59–124. San Francisco: Ignatius, 2011.

Geertz, Clifford. *The Interpretation of Cultures.* New York: Basic, 1973.

Goodman, Lenn. *Creation and Evolution.* New York: Routledge, 2010.

Guthrie, Jill. *Princeton University Art Museum: Handbook of the Collections.* Princeton, NJ: Princeton University Press, 2007.

Huizinga, Johan. *Homo Ludens: A Study of the Play Element in Culture.* New York: Beacon, 1955.

Hume, David. *Dialogues and Natural History of Religion.* Oxford: Oxford University Press, 2008.

McCarthy, Thomas. *Race, Empire, and the Idea of Human Development.* Cambridge: Cambridge University Press, 2009.

Meilaender, Gilbert C. *The Theory and Practice of Virtue.* Notre Dame, IN: University of Notre Dame Press, 1984.

Momigliano, Arnaldo. *Alien Wisdom: The Limits of Hellenization.* Cambridge: Cambridge University Press, 1971.

Plato. *The Laws.* Translated by Thomas L. Pangle. New York: Basic, 1980.

Ratzinger, Joseph. *Principles of Catholic Theology.* San Francisco: Ignatius, 1989.

Simon, Yves. *The Tradition of Natural Law: A Philosopher's Reflections.* New York: Fordham University Press, 1999.

Smith, Christian. *What is a Person? Rethinking Humanity, Social Life, and the Moral Good from the Person Up.* Chicago: University of Chicago Press, 2010.

Thompson, Michael. *Life and Action: Elementary Structures of Practice and Practical Thought.* Cambridge, MA: Harvard University Press, 2008.

www.ingramcontent.com/pod-product-compliance
Lightning Source LLC
Chambersburg PA
CBHW030309100426
42812CB00002B/626